"*Future Work* provides timely insight on the kind of culture that organizations need to meet the expectations of today's workforce. It will be useful for executives who want to learn how business must adapt to the revolution in work practices now being fuelled by incredibly rapid technological and social changes."
– **Stewart D. Friedman**, *Practice Professor at The Wharton School and author of Total Leadership*

"The world of work is changing rapidly and the office is undergoing a radical redesign to accommodate 21st-century work practices. This book captures these critical changes and identifies the leadership culture required to support them. It should be read by all managers who are striving to get the best results from their workforce in today's challenging economic climate."
– **Professor Ginny Gibson**, *Deputy Dean, Henley Business School*

"The business case for a flexible work environment is clear. Maitland and Thomson take this to the next level by explaining how organizations and managers can rethink their work cultures to retain their top talent and boost their productivity. This book is a must-read for managers and leaders."
– **Sylvia Ann Hewlett**, *author of Winning the War for Talent in Emerging Markets: Why Women Are the Solution*

"This is an exciting but daunting time as the way we work and the nature of employment are undergoing a revolution. The global economic turmoil means that previous experience of how things are done is no longer a reliable guide to the future. This book is perfectly timed to provide managers with a better understanding of how to successfully deliver tomorrow's working culture and workplace. The emphasis on the human side of these radical changes is particularly valuable."
– **Paul Bartlett**, *Chairman, Office Productivity Network*

"Overcoming the status quo and challenging outdated attitudes need not be as daunting as it might sound. *Future Work* draws on Alison and Peter's deep knowledge of the field, augmented by current case studies and survey evidence to provide a readable, practical, and comprehensive handbook that I can recommend highly."
– **Dr Anne Marie McEwan**, *CEO, The Smart Work Company*

"The nature of how, why, and where we work is changing, and this has repercussions for growth, sustainability, infrastructure, diversity, technology, and much more. Alison Maitland and Peter Thomson's book is where every board member and senior executive should start when thinking through the best way to future-proof their organization."
– **Lucy P. Marcus**, *CEO, Marcus Venture Consulting, and non-executive board director*

"*Future Work* should be required reading for every manager today. The way we work is changing rapidly and successful organizations must understand the advantages and challenges of the new ways of working."
– **Kate Lister**, *President, Telework Research Network*

"Alison and Peter have successfully navigated the future of work to explain why this is now a critical issue for all business leaders. Their book is essential reading for anyone wanting to gain a glimpse of the future and understand the new world of work."
– **Philip Ross**, *CEO, Unwork.com*

FUTURE WORK

HOW BUSINESSES CAN ADAPT AND THRIVE IN THE NEW WORLD OF WORK

ALISON MAITLAND
AND **PETER THOMSON**

First published 2011 by
PALGRAVE MACMILLAN

Palgrave Macmillan in the UK is an imprint of Macmillan Publishers Limited,
registered in England, company number 785998, of Houndmills, Basingstoke,
Hampshire RG21 6XS.

Palgrave Macmillan in the US is a division of St Martin's Press LLC,
175 Fifth Avenue, New York, NY 10010.

Palgrave Macmillan is the global academic imprint of the above companies
and has companies and representatives throughout the world.

Palgrave® and Macmillan® are registered trademarks in the United States,
the United Kingdom, Europe and other countries.

ISBN 978–0–230–28422–7

This book is printed on paper suitable for recycling and made from fully
managed and sustained forest sources. Logging, pulping and manufacturing
processes are expected to conform to the environmental regulations of the
country of origin.

A catalogue record for this book is available from the British Library.

A catalog record for this book is available from the Library of Congress.

10   9   8   7   6   5   4   3   2   1
20   19   18   17   16   15   14   13   12   11

Printed and bound in Great Britain by
CPI Antony Rowe, Chippenham and Eastbourne

For David, Eleanor and Isabel
(AM)
For Zac, Eva and all their generation
(PT)

CONTENTS

Contents

LIST OF ILLUSTRATIONS AND FIGURES

Illustrations

Figures

FOREWORD

For me, it was a toddler's exercise class that brought home the importance of workplace flexibility. It was 25 years ago, and the toddler was my two-year-old son. I was at a Gymboree class in our neighborhood – with my son and 24 mothers and their kids – because my wife had suggested our son would benefit from going, and that I would benefit from taking him. So every Wednesday morning, from 9 to 11, through the busiest time of year at the office, I was there in a track suit, playing, not working.

As the only father in the class I was a curiosity. Three weeks in, one of the mothers asked me what I did for a living. What job was so flexible that I could spend every Wednesday morning with my boy? When I told her I was an accountant she was shocked.

Why should she have been so surprised? I could organize my week around a Wednesday morning class. Even during our busiest period I could meet my deadlines, spend time with my son, and be happier, more productive and more well-rounded because of it. But 25 years ago, taking advantage of flexibility was an oddity.

I had another lesson about the importance of flexibility ten years ago. I was in my current role in Ernst & Young and we had a problem: women were leaving us at a much higher rate than men. We did all kinds of research to find out why. Was it pay? Benefits? Was our culture sexist? No. The biggest factor was that women felt that our workplace needed more flexibility.

So we changed. If people wanted to work different schedules we stopped asking them 'why?' and started asking their managers 'why not?'. Flexibility became more a 'right for all', not a 'privilege for few'. The results were dramatic. A year later we were retaining far more women. But we were retaining far more men, too, and more of our highest performers among both.

I'm convinced flexibility will become ever more important. The members of Generation Y joining the workforce expect it. They are highly committed workers – but don't want to be chained to their desks.

As Alison and Peter point out in this important book, organizations that give their workers more control over their time, provide them with more autonomy and empower them to use their skills and knowledge will be the winners in the twenty-first century. For many organizations and managers this requires a shift in culture and mindset. For those who are wondering where to start, I recommend this book.

James S. Turley – Chairman and CEO, Ernst & Young

Acknowledgments

The future of work and the changing workforce have been central to our respective careers for many years. When we embarked on this book, we wanted to combine our knowledge of writing about and advising on these important topics in a book that would help leaders and managers to make the shift to the brave new world of work.

During the course of our research, we found examples of this transition happening in many parts of the world, including the rising economies. While we knew some technology companies to be pioneers, we have discovered a wide range of other organizations that are leading the way and demonstrating that it can be done in many different sectors.

Our book has been enriched by the experience of the many executives and experts who generously gave us their time, and we also thank all the people who helped arrange interviews. We are grateful to those leaders who shared their personal stories about challenging and changing their own assumptions and then tackling resistance in others.

We would also like to thank the people who have helped us in many other ways, including: Shirley Borrett at the Telework Association; Fleur Bothwick at Ernst & Young; Janine Duchar at The Conference Board; Ellen Galinsky and Kelly Sakai at the Families and Work Institute; Alison Gregory, Sarah Williams-Gardener and colleagues at IBM; Kate Grussing at Sapphire Partners; Sarah Jackson at Working Families; Kate Lister and Tom Harnish at the Telework Research Network; Anne Madden and colleagues at the Equality and Human Rights Commission; Colin Maitland; Professor Ian Maitland at the University of Minnesota's Carlson School of Management; Caroline Waters at BT; and Stuart Woollard at King's College, London.

We are grateful to Cass Business School and Henley Business School, to which we are respectively affiliated, for their great help in disseminating our survey to their alumni networks. We would like to thank Lindsay Allen and Margrete Resellmo for their advice and assistance with the survey during their MBA studies at Henley and Cass.

Eleanor Davey Corrigan and Stephen Rutt at Palgrave Macmillan have been strong supporters of our project from the start, and we are most grateful for their enthusiasm, encouragement and advice.

Finally, and most importantly, we thank our families for their support, patience and love during the long months of researching, writing and editing. We hope this book will benefit people currently at work of every kind, as well as future generations.

Alison Maitland and Peter Thomson

CHAPTER 1

Time for change

Bram Meulenbeld and Martijn van der Linden, both in their early 30s, started out in traditional high-flying corporate careers, working for ING bank and Philips among other employers. During the global economic crisis, each concluded it was time for a change. 'I didn't want to go to an office all my life,' says van der Linden.

The two Dutch friends heard about a young firm called Amplify Trading in London's Canary Wharf that recruits people to trade financial futures electronically from wherever they are located. In 2009, they moved to a remote chalet high in the Austrian Alps, enjoying mountain sports in the mornings and switching on their computers in the afternoons to earn a living by trading shares on the New York stock exchange. They worked for as much or as little time each day as it took to make enough money.

A year later, they moved back to the Netherlands to embark on new careers in sustainable development. Bram set up a consultancy and web-site, Martijn turned to writing a book, both working mainly from their homes.

Bram says he is grateful that he can work in a way that would not have been possible 20, or even 10, years ago. 'I decided that "structured" life in an organization did not meet my requirements. I moved to Austria to benefit from two valuable things in life: a very interesting and challenging job and at the same time being able to fully benefit from all the things I value in life.

'Now, as I'm working from home, I can offer lower hourly tariffs because I don't have an expensive office. I use all kinds of online tools – Skype, Dropbox, Prezi – to work with others, while having all the freedom that I want around my work.' [1]

We are living in a time of exponential technological change. All around us there is evidence of digital breakthroughs. Whether it's an octogenarian ordering groceries online, a student updating a Facebook page or a celebrity entertaining fans through Twitter, the Web and its applications have rapidly and fundamentally altered our lives. They are having a profound effect on the way we communicate, learn and socialize. You may well be reading this book electronically on a Kindle, iPad or other such device.

As the experience of Bram and Martijn illustrates, there is enormous scope for the way in which we work to change as well. Some companies are responding by radically rethinking how they organize and manage people. They are at the forefront of a revolution in how we work. But they are still in the minority.

Many organizations remain stuck with a model of employment and management practices that were appropriate for work in the nineteenth and twentieth centuries, but not for the twenty-first. People are still expected to be present at their workplace for fixed periods of time and are paid by the hour, day, week or month for turning up. Long hours are often required and rewarded without any measure of the productivity involved. Getting the job done in half the time and going home early, instead of winning people praise, is more likely to see them sidelined as 'slackers'.

Yet there is overwhelming evidence that employees are more productive if they have greater autonomy over where, when and how they work. It should not be surprising to find that people feel motivated to produce their optimum when they are trusted to manage their own work patterns. There is nothing new in the concept of empowering employees. Progressive management thinkers have been preaching this since the middle of the last century.

What is new is that we now have the technology to enable a major shift in the way people work. It has already transformed how hundreds of thousands of self-employed individuals carry out their jobs. But few large organizations have fully grasped how to make the transition to more efficient business, better working lives and a healthier planet.

Fifty years ago, Douglas McGregor, the MIT management professor, wrote in *The Human Side of Enterprise*: 'Many managers would agree that the effectiveness of their organizations would be at least doubled if they could discover how to tap the unrealized potential present in their human resources.'[2] Managers often pay lip service to his proposition that people tend to be self-motivated and that management by empowerment is more effective than command-and-control (McGregor's Theory Y versus Theory X). When it comes to putting it into practice, however, old habits die hard.

In this book, we challenge those old habits. We explain why they have to change if companies are to keep pace with the competition in the networked world. Drawing on a wide body of research and on interviews with organizations at the leading edge, we reveal the culture, approaches and skills required to make the transition to more effective ways of managing people and organizing work for the overall benefit of business, individuals and society.

The new workforce

There are powerful reasons why companies and managers need to think differently about people and work. Tectonic shifts are taking place in the composition of the workforce, and in attitudes in wider society, which demand a response from any organization that wants to secure talent for the future, as we explain in **Chapter 2**.

Women now make up between 40 percent and 50 percent of the workforce in most developed countries,[3] as well as half or more of the employees inside many organizations. They represent the majority of the educated talent pool – around six out of ten graduates coming out of universities in the developed world, and a rising force in many parts of the developing world too.[4]

As women's earning power grows to equal or even outstrip that of their partners, the other side of the coin is that more men are taking on greater responsibility for childcare and are willing to be active fathers. In the US, the conflict between work and family commitments, felt acutely by working women during the late twentieth century, is now shared by men in dual-income families[5]. In the UK, fathers and mothers who were questioned about what would most help in achieving a better balance in their lives wanted 'a wider range of flexible job opportunities in all types of jobs' – a finding mirrored in the Shriver Report, *A Woman's Nation*, in the US.[6]

The presidency of Barack Obama has given impetus to pressure for a change in the working model in the US. In March 2010, Obama and his wife Michelle hosted a forum for labor leaders, CEOs, small business owners and policy experts to share ideas and strategies to create and encourage flexible workplaces, primarily to meet the needs of working families.

The fact is that the traditional male career model – which assumes people would have an unbroken full-time career and a steady rise to a peak of performance and earning power in their late 40s or 50s, followed by retirement around 60 – does not fit the new majority of the workforce.

Our aging societies pose both a huge challenge and an opportunity for better ways of working. From Japan and Australia to Italy and Germany, countries are grappling with how to support a generation of old people as the population of working age shrinks and fewer young people enter the workforce. The extension of working life is now inevitable in many parts of the world to maintain pensions and old-age care at acceptable levels.

Fortunately for governments and employers, this extension of work-ing life coincides with a desire on the part of many mature people to work past traditional retirement age, whether for financial reasons or to stay active and fulfilled. Many of them do not want to work in the old way, however, with fixed, full-time hours. Research shows, for example, that American baby boomers, the oldest of whom are now past 65, want greater control, autonomy and choice about where, how and when they work.[7]

This is a desire they share with others, notably the youngest people in work. This youthful cohort, often termed 'Generation Y', takes the greater flexibility afforded by technology for granted. They have grown up with the means to connect with their peers anytime anywhere, and they expect to be able to work this way too. Young 'knowledge workers' are as likely to want to work while munching a sandwich over their laptop in a wireless-enabled café as behind a desk in a traditional office.

Some business leaders have woken up to the huge significance of these cross-generational shifts, recognizing that a failure to meet the needs and expectations of the new workforce puts companies at risk of losing increasing numbers of able, skilled people.

Murray Martin, CEO of Pitney Bowes, the US provider of mail systems and services, is one of the leaders who understand this common thread unit-ing at least three of the four generations (veterans, baby boomers, Gen X and Gen Y) now in the workforce.

'For the veteran generation, they figure they've worked hard and have earned the right for more flexibility,' he told a business meeting, cit-ing the book Love 'Em or Lose 'Em by Beverly Kaye and Sharon Jordan-Evans.[8]

'Baby boomers are looking for more flexibility and structure to their workdays, and are rethinking their previously held "live to work" philos-ophy. The Gen X employee works to live, and Gen Y just assumes there is flexibility. These workers want to make a difference in the world and strive to strike a balance between their work and external lives.'

Martin pointed out that overstretched employees are prone to illness and unhappiness, while those who have greater autonomy are more commit-ted, productive and healthier. Flexible working interventions that increase worker control are likely to have a positive effect on health, according to a study of ten research projects in 2010.[9] Another report, looking at over 24,000 IBM employees worldwide, found that those with workplace flex-ibility could work an additional 19 hours per week before experiencing the same level of conflict between their work and personal lives as their office-bound counterparts.[10]

Expressing concern about the business world's generally sluggish reaction to these trends, Martin said: 'The corporate response is one that doesn't really want to hear it. But then (these corporations) can't understand why they're losing their best talent.'

Motivation is more than money

Demographic shifts, globalization and cost-cutting have already led to significant changes in the contractual models between employer and employee, with the growth of temporary agency work and the rise in part-time jobs in regions like Europe.

New models of network-based and virtual companies are springing up to challenge incumbent, or 'legacy', organizations by offering competitive rates based on their relatively low overheads and lack of hierarchy. These firms often assemble individuals or teams to work on specific projects and then disperse and regroup, giving the workers a high level of autonomy but lower job security than traditional employment contracts.

'As our society moves towards a knowledge-based economy, there will be an increasing individualization of people's behavior,' says Denis Pennel, managing director of the European Confederation of Private Employment Agencies.[11] The future, he points out, may look like something of a throwback to the past – to the pre-Industrial Revolution era when most workers, such as farmers, artisans and shopkeepers, were self-employed. In the information age, this individualization of work is leading both the self-employed and employed to use electronic media, such as LinkedIn, Second Life and Twitter, to meet, collaborate, market their ideas and socialize. Pennel says a new 'Social Contract' is needed to protect the rights of working people, regardless of their employment relationship.

One of the chief preoccupations of business leaders is how to attract, motivate and retain skills and talent. The excesses uncovered by the global financial crisis have triggered a fundamental questioning of reward and motivation, management styles and dominant models of work. It is perhaps no coincidence that the investment banks at the heart of the crisis were among the most extreme proponents of command-and-control management, short-term results and huge rewards, with the expectation of exceptionally long hours and 'face-time'.

Post-crisis, more people are questioning the conventional view that success is measured by the size of one's salary or bonus. There is discontent, even outrage, at the high rewards that executives receive, especially in the financial sector, as drastic government measures to reduce budget deficits begin to bite. There is also more awareness of the environmental impact of different industries and evidence that younger employees are choosing their employers based on their sustainability record.

A new branch of social science, the economics of happiness, is attracting increasing interest. Ever since Abraham Maslow introduced his Hierarchy of Needs in 1943, psychologists have been studying how people gain satisfaction in life. As Richard Layard points out in his book *Happiness*,[12] we are no happier now than we were 50 years ago, even though our incomes have doubled. The 'Happiness Index' produced by City & Guilds, a UK vocational education body, underlines how money does not buy happiness. 'For the last five years, sky-high salaries have rated pretty low on our list of reasons for feeling fulfilled and satisfied in our careers,' it says.[13]

Given the urgent need for talent and skills, many organizations are worried about the big challenge they face in keeping employees motivated and committed. Fewer than one in three employees worldwide is fully 'engaged' with their work, according to a report by the global consulting firm BlessingWhite.[14] Nearly one in five is 'disengaged', meaning that they only stay for the paycheck, not for the other things they need from work nor for what they could contribute in terms of discretionary effort. Engagement levels range from 37 percent in India to just 17 percent in China, with Europe at 30 percent and North America at 33 percent.

Research indicates that both baby boomers and the young workers of Gen Y, particularly in advanced economies, place at least as much importance on having flexible work, high-quality colleagues, recognition and access to new challenges as they do on financial rewards.[15]

Rewarding work, not time

An important way to motivate people is to trust them with greater autonomy over how they get work done. Doing so will reap dividends for managers and organizations, as the many case studies featured throughout the book demonstrate.

What we are proposing goes beyond arrangements typically known as 'flexible working'. Since the turn of the twenty-first century there has been a surge of interest in alternative working practices. The topic is moving from being a curiosity represented by a few supposedly quirky companies such as Semco in Brazil or Happy Computers in the UK to being part of mainstream human resources management.

The trouble is that most cases of flexible working have simply been grafted on to existing management practices without reviewing or changing the underlying model of work and careers. This has resulted in an uncomfortable coexistence between traditional management attitudes and pockets of greater flexibility, as we describe in **Chapter 3**.

Practices such as part-time work, compressed working weeks, job shares and term-time working do not challenge the prevailing, but now outdated and unsuitable, model of work. These cosmetic arrangements are introduced as an employee benefit and are commonly viewed by operational managers as a cost and an imposition. They are not seen as a business initiative to increase competitiveness and improve the bottom line.

So, in the second decade of the twenty-first century, we still live in a world where the predominant form of employment is 'fixed time and place'. This was established at the time of the Industrial Revolution when the factory clock dictated the rhythms of the day, replacing daylight and seasons from previous eras.

This model is based on time: If you give me your time to perform a job, I will reward you per hour. If you are a 'part-time' person and work less than the normal hours, you will be rewarded pro rata. The hours of work are set down in a contract issued by the employer, accepted by the employee and enforced by managers.

Many employers now offer varieties of 'flexi-time', allowing employees to vary their starting and finishing time around a set of core hours. But this is still a time-based relationship where the commodity being purchased is hours. What is achieved during those hours is of secondary importance. In many business cultures, people are expected to work far longer than the contracted hours. By doing so, they are seen as 'loyal', 'dedicated' and 'hard working' and are rewarded and promoted for this.

The concept of paying for time implies that people give up their freedom in exchange for money. They no longer have control over what they do between 9 a.m. and 5.30 p.m. from Monday to Friday – or 7 a.m. and 9 p.m. if they work in a high-pressure job. They need permission to go to the dentist, attend a funeral or take a holiday. They have the impossible task of taking their children to school at the same time as they are supposed to be getting to work and they end up in traffic congestion caused by everyone else trying to do the same thing.

No wonder that in Britain, for example, self-reported work-related stress, depression or anxiety accounted for an estimated 9.8m lost working days in 2009/10.[16] Or that in Australia, 60 percent of working women and nearly half of working men feel consistently time-pressured, and most workers would rather have two weeks' extra holiday than an equivalent pay rise.[17]

Paying people by the hour is the opposite of rewarding productivity. If you work slowly to perform a task, you will get paid more than if you work quickly. If your lawyer takes two hours to sort out your legal problem, you will pay her twice as much as if she fixes it in an hour. If the plumber takes three hours to mend a leak, he gets paid more than the efficient one who does it in an hour.

This system even encourages people to slow down their rate of work during 'normal' hours so that a job runs over into 'unsocial' hours and they are paid a higher rate to compensate for the extra hours. What's more, when people are paid for a fixed number of hours per week, as happens in the vast majority of organizations, working efficiently and completing tasks quickly results in being given more work to fill up the hours.

So, while 'flexible working' is a step toward a more sensible approach to work, it misses a fundamental point. Who is responsible for making sure that work gets done? If it is up to management to divide work into jobs and allocate these to people in return for a number of hours of their labor, we will remain stuck in an Industrial Age model of work. If a group of people agree on what they are going to achieve, then each carries out the tasks necessary to provide the results required, we have a new approach to work and management.

This new approach is well-suited for what Gary Hamel, the influential business thinker and writer, calls 'the creative economy', in which ideas are the basis of competitive advantage and management is about creating an environment in which people feel free to take the initiative, make connections and seize opportunities without waiting for direction.

It involves a radical change in the way work is done, rewarding people for their ideas and output, not for their time. Some organizations that have already made the change, or are in the process of doing so, call this 'smart' or 'agile' working because it makes sense for business as well as being good for people. We call it 'future work', because it represents the way that successful businesses of all kinds will operate in the future, not just in terms of the IT that supports the change, but crucially in terms of the way that work is organized and people are managed. Throughout the book, we feature international examples of organizations, large and small, private and public sector, pointing the way to the future.

Capturing hearts, minds and wallets

A key argument in favor of these new ways of working is that they improve productivity, a point we demonstrate in **Chapter 4**, where we examine why future work makes business sense. Countless surveys have shown big improvements in output when people have greater autonomy over how, where and when they carry out their work to meet their objectives.

This is a persuasive argument for managers to use in countering skepticism about the new work model. As long as practices such as working from home are seen simply as an employee benefit, they will not be treated seriously, especially by business leaders. However, when it becomes clear that they are major contributors to business success, attitudes change. As John D. Finnegan, CEO of Chubb, the US insurance group, told the *Financial Times*, he was initially skeptical about reported benefits but then changed his mind. 'As most CEOs would, I saw it as an employee accommodation program with a cost. I didn't know you could at the same time maintain or increase productivity.'[18]

The trigger for making a radical shift in the organizations we have studied is usually a business need – the soaring cost of real estate, a drive to improve customer service or a focus on reducing high rates of employee turnover. The benefits do not have to be confined to 'knowledge work', although this type of work is easiest to transform through communications technology. Jobs in many sectors, such as health care and retailing, have to be done in a fixed location, while others, in manufacturing for example, require people to be available at fixed times of the day or night. But even these jobs contain tasks, such as form filling and record keeping, that are susceptible to far greater autonomy than is currently exercised.

In addition to productivity, the business benefits of future work include major cost savings on real estate and on employee turnover and absenteeism, extended customer service cover and the ability to enter new markets faster. There are less obvious advantages, such as a lower risk of business disruption and more transparent succession planning. There are also important benefits for the environment and wider society, which in turn contribute to the green credentials and public image of the organization.

The global economic crisis has brought urgency to the drive for change. Organizations have been forced to focus even harder on costs. Many resorted to shorter working weeks on reduced pay as a way to preserve jobs during the recession. Shorter-lived crises, such as the 2009 swine flu outbreak, the recent harsh winters in the northern hemisphere and the closure of airspace due to volcanic ash from Iceland, have highlighted the benefits of technology at work. Companies that equipped people to work from home or on the move experienced far less disruption than the rest. In the post-crisis period, the savings associated with a shift to future work offer employers a further opportunity to improve growth while keeping a lid on costs.

Leadership 2.0

Much has been written about 'enterprise 2.0' technologies – the web of devices, services and applications that enable organizations and people to work more collaboratively and efficiently in the internet era. Cloud computing is being heralded as the next stage of this evolution that will change the way we work. Technology often provides the essential underpinning, but the key to moving to a more efficient and healthier working model is a change in culture, led from the top of the organization.

This book is about the human side of the transition to future work. Rather than 'enterprise 2.0', it is about 'leadership 2.0' and 'management 2.0'. It is aimed at leaders and managers who want to equip themselves with the thinking and skills needed to meet the challenges of the new world of work.

The global crisis triggered fevered debate about the leadership of our largest institutions, particularly in the financial sector. The economic repercussions of the financial earthquake left trust in business leadership at a low ebb. Only about half of employees in Europe and North America trust the people at the top of their organization, who represent the culture and values and who need to inspire performance and commitment, according to the BlessingWhite survey.[19] Rebuilding this badly damaged trust will take innovative approaches as well as time.

Many of today's senior managers rose to the top by working long hours in full-time jobs. They have reaped the rewards of that system. The not so subtle message to others is that if they want to climb 'the ladder' of success, they too must follow traditional career paths and make the necessary 'sacrifices'. The mantra is that senior jobs in high-performing companies require near total commitment of body and soul, and that balance at these high levels is virtually impossible.

Yet the crisis has demonstrated more clearly than ever how essential it is to have balanced, responsive leaders at the top of companies to avoid a repeat of the disasters that brought whole institutions crashing to oblivion. The prevailing work model at the top is not a healthy way to live, to lead or to maintain perspective – witness the surveys showing high levels of stress among managers, as well as staff. It also sends a negative message to many aspiring leaders: Don't expect to have any control over your lives if you choose to climb the ladder to the executive suite.

Will the talented individuals joining the workforce today be prepared to play this game? There is increasing evidence to show that they – and many of those already in the workforce – will not. This will leave an ever-shrinking pool of potential leaders, with more of the best talents leaking out of larger organizations.

'Leadership in the past was built on organizational power and the ability to dish out money,' says Damien O'Brien, head of Egon Zehnder International, the executive search firm. 'This new generation coming through will have less deference to organizational power and for many of them money will be less of a driver. They will come to work if they are inspired. The successful leaders of the future will be those who enable their people to release their creativity, rather than trying to control what they do.'[20]

The biggest component missing from leadership today – especially in the corporate world – is women. If diversity in the leadership team really is a strategic objective, as more and more business leaders claim, then the requirement of 'total commitment' will undermine it. It will perpetuate the exclusion, or self-exclusion, of a large part of the talent that companies need to survive and thrive. This, in turn, will encourage 'groupthink' – the pressure within a homogenous group to go along with the prevailing arguments rather than rock the boat – and the damaging effects we saw during the global crisis.

Christine Lagarde, as finance minister of France, was an eloquent and well-placed contributor to the debate on the need for a new and healthier model of capitalism. 'The current economic crisis affords us an opportunity to impose more responsible, moderate and equitable approaches to finance,' she wrote in an *International Herald Tribune* opinion piece entitled 'Women, Power and the Challenge of the Financial Crisis'.[21] 'I am determined to do everything within my power to change the rules of the game and do my best to ensure that a crisis such as this can never happen again.'

A fresh approach to leadership is essential if organizations are to break free from the old rules of work. In our research for this book, we found a small but growing band of leaders who have had the courage to challenge and change these rules, not only by encouraging future work in their teams but also by remodeling their own career and work patterns. Future work is for everyone. Indeed, it is important that leaders, including those responsible for running large businesses, show how it can be done, as they are the most powerful agents of change. We tell these trailblazing leaders' stories in **Chapter 5**.

Leaders and managers who set goals for people and trust them to achieve those goals will encourage others at every level to take on responsibility and generate positive outcomes for the organization. This will lead to power being distributed through the company, rather than simply being concentrated at the top. Diversity, as research studies show, is important to creativity and innovation. Future work will enable a more diverse group of people, from different backgrounds and with different perspectives and talents, to flourish and move into leadership positions.

Under new management

For many of today's managers, these shifts are likely to be a challenge, since they require a willingness to examine and probably change aspects of their own management style, as many of those we interviewed have done. It may feel uncomfortable. But it produces significant results and it is already happening in companies at the forefront of the new world of work. In **Chapter 6**, we explore the role of location in future work, and the implications for management methods as teams become dispersed across locations and time zones, and as offices shift from workplaces to meeting places.

Traditionally, managers have been responsible for the allocation of tasks to their people. They have decided what needs to be done, by when and by whom. They have monitored progress and used various motivational techniques to encourage their staff to perform effectively. The whole process has been based on the assumption that the manager knows best and has the authority to tell people what to do.

Yet for the past 50 years, respected management writers have been arguing that motivation is about giving people responsibility and creating an environment where they can use their skills to achieve something satisfying. Maslow, Frederick Herzberg and McGregor were preaching this in the 40s, 50s and 60s and Charles Handy, Peter Drucker and Tom Peters were pushing the same messages in the 80s and 90s.

As Dan Pink puts it in his enlightening book *Drive*, a number of recent behavioral science studies show that 'autonomous motivation promotes greater conceptual understanding, better grades, enhanced persistence at school and in sporting activities, higher productivity, less burnout and greater levels of psychological wellbeing. Those effects carry over to the workplace.'[22] It is about trusting people to get on with their work and giving them real freedom of choice as to how they do the job. It is about rewarding success, not punishing failure. In summary it is about treating people as adults and not as children.

We carried out a survey of international alumni of Cass Business School and Henley Business School in the UK, as well as other managers around the world, to investigate what kind of organizational cultures enable future work to thrive.

Our key findings are that:

- A majority of managers expect there to be a revolution in working practices in the next decade
- Most managers think their organizations are not adapting fast enough to new ways of working
- A majority want more freedom to let people manage their own work patterns
- More than half believe new ways of working would benefit their business

- Organizations that enable future work tend to have a strong culture of trust, to value individual creativity and input and to treat people as self-motivated

Based on these findings, we explain in **Chapter 7** what kind of culture organizations need to foster to adapt and thrive in the new world of work. We also examine how countries and regions vary widely in their openness to new working practices, although the desire for a different deal from work is not peculiar to employees in advanced industrial societies.

The number of hours worked each year gives an indication of the differing approaches to work among developed nations. According to OECD figures, people work an average of 1389 hours per year in the Netherlands while at the other extreme in South Korea the average is 2256 hours.[23] This means that more than three Dutch workers are needed to match the hours worked by two Koreans. There is a distinct difference in approach between many European Union (EU) countries, which are restricted by the Working Time Directive, and the US, where there is no regulation. Both genders in the US work on average 41 hours a week. In Europe, women work just over 30 hours, compared with around 38 hours for men.[24]

In addition to our unique survey, we have interviewed over 60 executives and experts in global businesses, medium-sized firms, start-ups and public sector organizations around the world. Drawing on our research and our knowledge of what works, we set out in **Chapter 8** the main principles for success and the key skills that managers need to make the transition to managing people in the new world of work.

This book is about a twenty-first century model of work that starts from the principle that people are involved in the process. It recognizes that employees have lives outside the workplace and allows for this in the creation and design of jobs. It is empowerment in practice.

The ultimate empowerment is self-employment. This gives an individual the freedom and the responsibility to get work done however they choose. So this is a good place to start when designing jobs for the future. Can the work be given to an individual who is totally self-managed, who charges for his or her output and who is responsible for his or her own time? There may be good reasons to keep the work in-house and give it to an employee. If so, can it nonetheless be done by someone who manages her or his own time?

If your organization starts from the basis that work is done in the office between fixed daytime hours, then you still have something close to a traditional work arrangement. If you believe that work – or at least parts of people's 'jobs' – can be done anywhere at any time, then you are moving toward future work.

In **Chapter 9**, we set out a guide to how to put this approach into practice. Leadership from the top is crucial, so it is important for senior management to understand and commit to the business case for change in their organization.

The steps that a manager can take include consulting his or her team on how they can best organize their work to improve their output. Using the fact that people are more productive when they have control over their own work patterns, the team can discuss how to achieve their business goals as well as enable healthier, more balanced lives.

Anand Pillai, senior vice president at HCL Technologies, the Indian IT services company that advocates putting employees first, says that it is an insult to their intelligence to recruit and train the best people and then tell them what to do. 'They have the knowledge, they have the resources, we just have to empower, engage and enable them to use it. That's the beauty of an intrapreneurial organization – people taking responsibility for doing the things we have entrusted them to do.' [25]

The key to successful implementation of future work is the measurement of output. By agreeing what needs to be achieved, managers can set their employees free from the constraints of 'presenteeism' – the belief that they must be present in the workplace, often for long hours, regardless of whether there is work to do – and allow them to work more productively.

Trusting people to act as adults, and enabling them to decide the best way to do their job, including the 'where' and 'when', is the secret of success. Organizations that have discovered this are now reaping the rewards. Those that have not are in danger of being overtaken by events.

For individual managers, the experience of implementing future work will depend heavily on the organizational culture, as our research shows. If you work in an environment where experimentation is encouraged and managers are able to try new ideas, it will be a positive experience. If complying with the status quo and maintaining corporate norms is the route to success, it will be an uphill battle. This should not stop you from trying, since by doing so you will be helping your business to adapt and thrive. Change is happening fast, faster than any other major changes in the history of work, and technology-enabled future work will not wait for those who fail to seize the opportunity now.

CHAPTER 2

How work has evolved

In a few hundred years, when the history of our time will be written from a long-term perspective, it is likely that the most important event historians will see is not technology, not the Internet, not e-commerce. It is an unprecedented change in the human condition. For the first time – literally – substantial and rapidly growing numbers of people have choices. For the first time, they will have to manage themselves. And society is totally unprepared for it.

Peter Drucker, 2000[1]

A historical shift

With his usual prescience, Peter Drucker, the father of modern management, foresaw the really important trend underlying the information age. At the turn of the twenty-first century, he recognized a historical shift in management and the place of work in society. He saw that people were faced with career choices unavailable to previous generations and women in particular had opportunities that never existed before.

Thanks to technology, we can now work in ways unimaginable 30 years ago. Social attitudes to work and life are shifting fast. Economic pressures are forcing employers to review the productivity and effectiveness of their human resources. The world of work is ripe for radical reform.

Yet, as Drucker said, we are unprepared for this shift toward self-management, which is a central element of future work. A decade after his prediction, much of the mainstream world of work still relies on Industrial Age working practices, and management practices reflect this. There are hierarchies, career paths and compensation plans to meet corporate targets. The underlying logic is clear: management knows best. Direction is set from the top and managers transmit the orders down the line. Employees are a resource to be used by the business to achieve its aims, typically to maximize the bottom line. Companies refer to people as 'human resources', but in practice struggle to find ways to account for them as assets rather than liabilities.

The last time work underwent a major transformation was the move from a world governed by the seasons and daylight to one ruled by the factory whistle and clock. In the middle of the nineteenth century, 90 percent of white men in the US worked for themselves as farmers, merchants, or craftsmen. The biggest company in Britain in 1850 had only 300 employees.

The next 50 years saw the rise of the first massive corporations that served us well during the twentieth century. Leaders perfected hierarchical, command-and-control management processes based on the examples set by the Army and the Church. Businesses improved efficiency by gaining economies of scale, standardizing work processes and introducing the production line. Work had moved from being an activity using an individual's skill, producing an output of value, to a job performing a narrow set of tasks in exchange for a salary.

Henry Ford's legacy

The model of work that developed over the past century reflects the thinking of Henry Ford. Whether people are employed in a factory, office, hospital or school, they are part of a production process. If the same product can be obtained with fewer people or lower pay, unit costs are reduced and profits improved. Companies have worked hard at reducing the cost of labor and increasing output. They standardized jobs to make them easily repeated, reduced the variety of tasks to increase the reliability of output and studied activities to the finest detail to eliminate waste and improve efficiency.

For a while this worked. The production line was the driver of industrialized economies and people were prepared to carry out routine work for low pay. Large corporations thrived and nations prospered, as long as economies of scale gave some competitive advantage. But 'Fordism' produced boring work, reduced to the simplest tasks, with the minimum possible discretion exercised by the worker. This bred militant unions who defended powerless employees against exploitation and even led to deliberate sabotage just to relieve the boredom.

'If there was a single question that obsessed twentieth century managers, from Frederick Taylor to Jack Welch, it was this: How do we get more out of our people?' writes Gary Hamel in *The Future of Management*.[2] 'At one level, this question is innocuous – who can object to the goal of raising human productivity? Yet it's also loaded with Industrial Age thinking: How do we (meaning "management") get more (meaning units of production per hour) out of our people (meaning the individuals who are obliged to follow our orders)? Ironically, the management model encapsulated in this question virtually guarantees that a company will never get the best out of its people. Vassals and conscripts may work hard, but they don't work willingly.'

In the age of what Hamel describes as the creative economy, knowledge work drives advanced nations. It is no longer necessary to gather people together in large organizations every day to ensure the smooth running of the wheels of commerce or the functions of government. Yet this is what still happens, because current management methods are based on an increasingly outdated model of work.

'Victorian factory culture' in City of London

Here's an example of 'anachronistic' working practices in the City of London, as described by a banker in his 50s who has spent his career in large financial institutions, and who preferred to remain anonymous.[3]

'The nineteenth century factory culture of being tied to one's desk is still strong,' he says. 'In a lot of European firms based in London, it's common for large sections of the workforce to be required at their desks between 7 a.m. and 7.30 a.m. Firms involved in equities markets feel they have to have people there for the Reuters news service releases of companies' results and stock exchange news from 7 a.m. It's questionable whether all of them are doing anything useful with that information in the following hour or so.

'While it makes business sense to be functioning when clients in continental Europe, operating an hour ahead, start work, it is not always rational to take long-term decisions based on short-term trading moves between 7 am. and 9 am. This is face time by management diktat. Managers feel that if their competitors are there and get the news at 7 a.m., they might lose ground if they don't match them. However, it does not follow that this information has to be received at a single location.'

At the other end of the day, some people feel they have to stay until the boss leaves. They may be busy, or they may just be killing time. This culture is particularly associated with Japanese firms, but it is widespread.

The banker argues that, while seeing colleagues regularly is important, it no longer needs to be five days a week. 'All the technology that has come into people's working lives over the past 20 to 30 years hasn't made much difference to the way bankers move around for work: when they aren't traveling for business, they go to the office.'

What needs to happen to trigger a change in working practices? 'If management set a different standard, for example that people are expected to be in the office three or four days out of five, with the norm being that you work from home one or two days a week, that would be a substantive change,' he replies. 'You need one or two market leaders to pioneer it and demonstrate its success and its impact on costs, either on measurable office space costs or on staffing costs as a result of improved morale and retention.'

Technology is not a panacea

The last 20 years have seen an explosion in the technologies available to support new ways of working. It is easy to forget that the personal computer was only invented in the 1980s and had limited use until the 1990s, when the advent of the Internet and the World Wide Web opened up the possibility of genuine personal computing. The first generation of cellular mobile phones was launched in the 1980s but it was not until the 1990s, when digital networks arrived, that usage really took off. Then in 2002, with the first 3G networks, it became practical to use cell phones for surfing the Internet and sending emails. So we should not be too surprised that innovative working practices enabled by these technologies are still in their infancy, with a long way to go to reach their full potential.

People have been able to work at home using dial-up technologies to exchange data since the 1970s, but it was not until the turn of the twenty-first century that broadband communications arrived. In the 1980s, there were a few teleworking pioneers, mainly in the rapidly expanding IT industry, who were experimenting with alternative work styles. Computer programmers were able to work from home and send their coding across a standard phone line via a modem. Some saw this at the time as a forerunner of the way most people would work in the future.

What has happened in reality has not lived up to the optimistic predictions from the 1980s. The growth of full-time home-based work has been relatively slow, while the expansion of part-time teleworking has been rapid in some countries. The UK's Office for National Statistics, for example, found that the total number of teleworkers in the UK increased by 65–70 percent between 1997 and 2001.[4] In the US, the number of employee telecommuters rose by 39 percent, from 12.4m in 2006 to 17.2m in 2008.[5] This growth was mainly in the 'Occasional Telecommuter' category, with the number who work remotely 'almost every day' staying static.

What has clearly changed from the early days of telework is the availability of technology to support a wide variety of jobs. Anyone involved in 'knowledge work' can now take advantage of affordable laptops, smartphones and broadband connections. We have moved rapidly from the pioneering days of computing, when the only users of IT were the technical specialists, to the age of universally available tools. People have also adopted the Web as a resource in their personal lives, for everything from finding information and shopping to organizing street protests. Surfing is done on the Internet as well as the waves, browsing on websites as well as in bookshops and chatting through social media as well as face-to-face in real cafés.

Yet we are far from mastering technology, either in terms of workplace innovation or in the way our work is integrated with our personal lives. On the one hand, communications technology in the home has advanced much more rapidly than in most workplaces. Look at the technology being used by the under 25s: at home they will be chatting to friends on Facebook, having live conversations with them via internet applications such as Skype, sending text messages, watching the latest uploads to YouTube and keeping an eye on the people they follow on Twitter. But when they go to work, they may well find that communications have barely advanced beyond email, that social media are blocked and that discussion forums are confined to the water cooler.

On the other hand, technology has allowed work to invade our personal territory. Take the example of the mobile phone. Its use has grown exponentially, with little or no adaptation to conventional working practices. So its capacity to connect people at times and places hitherto out of reach has meant that additional working time has simply been layered onto what was already required. Its power quickly became a double-edged sword. Managers could now call their employees when they were traveling across the country or around the world. Customers could contact their suppliers at any time to demand a better service. People could be tracked down at weekends or on vacation for 'urgent' business.

When email capability arrived on handheld devices, conventional working hours stretched further. In 2006, the new term 'Crackberry', depicting the addictive qualities of BlackBerrys and other handheld devices, was named the word of the year by the staff at Webster's New World College Dictionary.[6]

Technology itself is neither the hero nor the villain in these developments. It can be used to liberate individuals and allow them to have more balanced lives. It can equally be used to extend work into times and places that people would prefer to reserve for their leisure. It can be a catalyst for new work styles that empower employees, but it can also be an instrument for the employer to monitor and control them more closely. It allows people to work more effectively but it can also distract them from their jobs. It improves communications, speeds up business processes and increases efficiency, but it can also turn jobs into boring repetitive tasks. It has turned call centers into the twentieth-century equivalent of the nineteenth-century factory, with people mindlessly following instructions.

So it is not the technology that changes our working lives, it is the way we choose to use it. A lot depends on whose finger, physically or metaphorically, controls the 'off' switch.

People's changing priorities

The rapid development of technology has run in parallel with major shifts in society. Attitudes to work and careers have evolved dramatically over the past 30 years. For many employees, especially in developed countries, life no longer revolves around work. Employers cannot just assume that people will accept standard conditions of employment and take working patterns as a given. If the job can be done without sticking to a rigid pattern of time and place, employees will expect flexibility to be on offer. If it is not, they are likely to look elsewhere.

In early 2010, the top benefit sought by professionals across the UK was flexible working, with almost half putting it top of their list, according to a survey carried out by PricewaterhouseCoopers.[7] Interestingly, it was given fairly equal priority by men and women. This survey also revealed disillusionment with the traditional career working for a major employer. Exactly half the respondents said they would prefer to work for themselves. Almost a third wanted to be employed by a company whose values matched theirs, while the remaining 20 percent said they wanted to work for an elite company that employed only the best.

Other countries are seeing similar trends. A survey of hourly paid workers in the US found that flexibility was an important factor in deciding to take the job for 83 percent of workers who had joined in the last two years. The survey by Corporate Voices for Working Families[8] also found that 60 percent of the workers said it was likely they would leave the company if they did not have the opportunity to work flexibly.

The workforce of today, therefore, has different expectations of their employers than previous generations had. They know they are unlikely to get job security and a safe pension in exchange for lifelong service. They are looking for fair rewards, flexibility and engaging work. Notions of what constitutes a successful career are inevitably changing too.

A survey of over 3200 Generation Y finance professionals across 122 countries found that lifestyle factors outweighed contractual ones in their choice of job. 'Perhaps the preference towards lifestyle factors is in part due to a changing definition of success,' says the report by ACCA, the professional accountants' body, and Mercer, the consulting firm. 'Our survey suggests the historical view of career success being defined by more money probably rings less true for this generation. This is a generation that seeks a much broader range of benefits from working life, and actively seeks out organizations that can deliver this.'[9]

As we pointed out in Chapter 1, large numbers of employees around the world are thoroughly disengaged from their work. A report by the Chartered Institute of Personnel and Development in the UK found that fewer than one in ten employees looked forward to going to work all of the time, and just over a quarter rarely or never looked forward to going to work. Younger employees were more disengaged than their older colleagues. Perhaps the most interesting finding was that people on flexible contracts felt much more positive about their managers than did non-flexible workers, 'most probably because managers who take the trouble to find ways of helping their staff manage their work–life balance are also those who have better general management skills'.[10]

Why are so many people disillusioned with work? Is it that the work is intrinsically boring, or is it to do with the way they are managed? We believe the answer is clear. How people are managed has not kept pace with their expectations. Attitudes toward work have changed but many management practices still reflect the model of work that prevailed in the twentieth century.

The role of gender

A generation or two ago, the world was arguably a much simpler place. Everyone knew where she or he belonged. Men went to work, but rarely did women pursue careers outside the home. Despite the vital role played by women when they took many men's jobs during two world wars, they were largely back at the hearth in the 1950s. Then came the Pill, the women's liberation movement, a raft of equal rights legislation and women's journey toward parity with men in the workplace.

It has been a long road. In the UK, the 1919 Sex Disqualification (Removal) Act allowed women to become lawyers, vets and civil servants. Even then, only single women could get a job in the British Civil Service and it was only after the Second World War that they were allowed to stay once they married. It was not until 1961 that Barclays Bank removed its marriage bar and it was still perfectly legal in the UK until 1975 to dismiss an employee for becoming pregnant.

Women in the US gained voting rights through the Nineteenth Amendment to the Constitution in 1920 but only in the 1960s were several federal laws improving the economic status of women passed. The Equal Pay Act of 1963 required equal wages for men and women doing equal work. The Civil Rights Act of 1964 prohibited discrimination against women by any company with 25 or more employees.

Within the lifetime of a senior manager, we have moved from a world where women were legally and socially treated as second-class citizens to one where they have equal employment rights and nearly equal representation in the labor force of many advanced economies. In countries with generous maternity benefits compared with paternity provisions, it can be argued that women have overtaken men in certain entitlements. Sex discrimination in employment is illegal in most Western countries and many have equal pay legislation to counteract the legacy of low-paid 'women's work', although this has not eradicated the pay gap.

The introduction of maternity leave and the right to return to work in the same or equivalent job is almost universal,[11] even though some employers still blatantly flout the law.

The US is one of the few countries in the world that does not mandate paid maternity leave, a fact that led the campaigning organization Human Rights Watch to publish a report in 2011 accusing it of 'failing its families'. The US Family and Medical Leave Act of 1993 provides for parental leave for serious medical conditions, but this is unpaid and does not cover all workers. Many countries provide paid paternity leave, but not the US. Yet countries that have paid family leave programs show productivity gains, reduced turnover costs and health care savings, according to Janet Walsh, deputy women's rights director at Human Rights Watch.[12]

The 1980s and 1990s saw a series of legislative changes in most Western countries that made employment fairer and increasingly 'family friendly'. These reflected changing attitudes in society toward work. No longer was it a male preserve. Women could have a career and a family. They could take their maternity leave and still return to their former position in the hierarchy. It seemed we were moving into a truly gender-neutral world of work.

Sadly, reality has not kept up with the ideals. Ironically, the very legislation that was designed to ensure fairer treatment for women reinforced some of the old stereotypes. Women had to be given 'special' treatment so they could take time off work to have children. Men might have the right to a few weeks of paternity leave if they were lucky, but maternity provisions were much longer and more generous. This has strengthened the notion that it is primarily women who have children, not women *and* men together. It has reinforced some employers' beliefs that it is a disadvantage to hire women of childbearing age.

Women are still underrepresented in many professions and in the ranks of senior management, despite over 40 years of equality legislation. It will be an uphill battle to achieve real equality as long as employment legislation and HR policies imply that mothers need special treatment and fathers do not. If we stop assuming that 'men have careers and women have children', we will achieve faster progress.

Scandinavian countries such as Norway and Sweden are leading the way, with generous parental leave for both mothers and fathers. Introducing parental rights that are shared completely would go a long way to breaking through the remaining prejudices. It would encourage fathers to take an active role in childcare and adjust their work patterns to accommodate family responsibilities. Employers would in future have to assume that any employee, male or female, might need to take a substantial amount of time for parental responsibilities at some point in their (increasingly long) working lives.

It does not help that maternity leave and flexible working legislation are often classified together as 'family friendly'. Employees in the UK, for example, were given a legal right to request flexible working from their employers in 2003. But this right only applied to parents of children up to the age of 6 or up to 18 for a disabled child. In 2006, this right was extended to anyone caring for an adult relative, and in 2009 the age for children was extended to 16. Parents and caregivers are identified as needing special treatment and requiring the weight of the law to persuade employers to listen to their requests.

We do not quarrel with the need for legislation to protect vulnerable employees from unscrupulous employers and to provide a baseline from which good employers can build far better practices. The difficulty lies in the framing of this type of legislation and the message it sends. Flexible working is seen as an employee accommodation involving a change to 'normal' working patterns. It reinforces the prejudice that provisions are forced on employers against their will and interfere with managers' ability to get their job done. As we shall see in Chapter 3, this is the opposite of what actually happens with new ways of working.

We need an urgent reframing of careers and career development, because women's career paths tend to be very different from the traditional male model that still prevails in many organizations. Companies cannot afford to continue losing so much female talent. More than half of the students now in universities worldwide are women, according to UNESCO.[13] In North America and Europe, a third more women than men are on campus. Latin America, the Caribbean and Central Asia also show high rates of female enrolments. In a number of countries, at least two females graduate for every male. These young women are going into employment and becoming well-established in their careers before even thinking of starting a family. By then they may well be earning more than their male partners.

There are signs of a big shift in men's attitudes to family and work, as the corollary of women's increasing participation in the workforce. In the US, employed fathers in dual-income couples are now significantly more likely to experience 'work–life conflict' than mothers, according to a report by the Families and Work Institute. Significantly, it found that the probability of this conflict increased with high job pressure, but decreased when men had greater autonomy in their jobs and greater support from their supervisors.[14]

Far more is known today about the importance for children's well-being of bonding with their fathers as well as their mothers. Sixty percent of parents in the UK think fathers should spend more time with their children, a survey by the Equality and Human Rights Commission found. Asked if they spent enough time with their own children, 44 percent of men and 23 percent of women said they did not. Half of fathers, and nearly a third of mothers, thought they spent too much time at work.[15]

'The way we "do" family has changed – not only because mothers are more likely to go out to work but also because today both mothers *and* fathers want close relationships with children as they are growing up,' says Dr Caroline Gatrell of Lancaster University Management School, who has been researching into fathers, work and family life for the UK charity Working Families.

Home for bedtime

Throughout his career, Ben Richardson, 35, has sought to control where and when he works as far as possible, whether in his first job in chartered accountancy, next co-managing an environmental asset management firm and subsequently as a consultant. 'I realized from an early age that you work for yourself, not someone else, even if you work for an organization,' he says. 'I've no problem with working hard or long hours when I'm working. For me, it's more that when I'm not working, I'm not working.'

Ben is married to a full-time barrister and they have two young children, so he has been contemplating swapping the flexibility of his independent contractor role for a full-time job. He says working within easy reach of his London home is so important that he would take a job paying half as much as one located at the other end of the country. The role and the culture of the company also matter. He would not, for example, go for a corporate finance role in a big investment bank 'whatever the salary', because it would mean sacrificing too much in terms of his life. 'I'd want at least 30 days' vacation a year and a place where I would be able to walk out at least twice a week, if not every day, and be home to put my children to bed.'

Young lawyers demand new approach

Starting out in business as a media sensation can do wonders for your employer branding. That was what happened when eight young Danish lawyers left their firms to set up Sirius, an all-purpose corporate law firm that promised to end the long-hours culture.

The four women and four men attracted positive press in 2006 for daring to go against the conventional working pattern of 60–70-hour weeks in favor of fewer hours and greater flexibility for all staff, including partners.

They were in tune with demographic and social trends. 'Within the past ten years, there's been an enormous shift in the approach of young lawyers,' says Birgit Gylling Andersen, an employment lawyer and founding partner. 'Now it's both male and female lawyers who discuss over lunch how to handle the kids, and both who take days off or leave to look after the children. Young lawyers are demanding a new approach.'

With 30 people, Sirius is now a medium-sized firm in Denmark. The media coverage ensured them a ready supply of lawyers keen to work for the firm, which keeps normal hours to about 45 per week and requires only 1100 billable hours per year per lawyer compared with an average of 1500–1600 in Danish law firms, she says.

'If you go through our office at 6 pm, it's very rare that there's more than one or two people left, and they are normally partners. If you do have to work long hours on a case, we say: "Take some time off". It's very important for our employees that they know it's acceptable to have personal wishes.'

How do corporate clients, who typically expect instant service from their well-paid legal advisers, react to the Copenhagen firm's working principles? 'There are challenges,' she acknowledges. 'But our clients are understanding of the way we work. They also have their personal needs. And we attract clients that also wish to work in a different way. A lot of modern corporate leaders want a different kind of lawyer. It's not just a question of working hours. It's a question of understanding their business and their values and being a partner in their decision process, rather than telling them what to do and how much it will cost, which is the old-fashioned way.'

Ms Gylling Andersen, who is part of a women business leaders' network in Denmark, says the firm's groundbreaking approach has attracted particular interest from 'female leaders who want to do things in a different way'.

Work and life across generations

Awareness of the tension between work and the rest of life has grown in recent decades in parallel with globalization, women's rising participation in the workplace and legislative developments. 'Work–life balance' was not in the management vocabulary until the 1990s. How people chose to spend their time outside work was not the business of their managers. Employees were used to fitting their personal lives round the fixed commitments of their jobs. Now all that has changed. With the 24/7 demands of business, good employers know they have to make allowances for employees' lives outside work if they want to attract and retain the best people.

We live in a shrinking world. Telephone enquiries from customers in the US and Europe are likely to be answered by call center staff in India or the Philippines. We take it for granted that we can shop for almost anything at almost any time. The Internet has delivered services to the home and revolutionized the retail sector and personal banking. Totally new ways of buying and selling products have emerged through channels such as eBay. So it is hardly surprising that young people in particular expect the way we work to be different too. If I can shop any time I choose, why can't I work any time I choose?

Inevitably some views about work differ across the generations. The contrast in life experience between baby boomers and Generation Y is obvious. People born in the decade after the Second World War went through school, university and their first jobs without ever seeing a computer, except behind the doors of an air-conditioned room. Yet people born since 1990 have never known a world without computers, cell phones and the Internet at their fingertips.

However, these 'bookend generations', as economist Sylvia Ann Hewlett and colleagues describe them, share some common views about work, apparently in contrast to Generation X sandwiched between them. Their research found that both generations are seeking a 'remixed' set of rewards. They prize meaning and choice over money. 'They are shedding Industrial Age conceptions of work and demanding control over when, where and how work gets done.'[16]

The baby boomers include many people who no longer want to fully retire. It may be that they feel they are just not ready for retirement at 60 or 65. However, it is increasingly likely that the pension fund they hoped would keep them going through their old age is grossly inadequate. We are emerging from the 'golden era' of pensions that guaranteed a percentage of final pay. Individuals increasingly have to take responsibility for saving for their retirement. Employers and pension providers are slowly waking up to the fact that the traditional 'cliff edge' between full-time work and full-time retirement no longer makes sense. Why should someone who still has a wealth of experience to give to their employer not continue to do so, at least on a flexible basis?

Some companies are tapping into this 'mature' talent. For example, HP, the global technology company, has a program to encourage retired employees to become 'ambassadors' and work, often unpaid, in their local PC store promoting HP products. In the UK, Domestic & General, an insurance company, uses 'age-positive' strategies to attract and keep older workers, employing around 700 people aged 16 to over 70.[17]

Life expectancy continues to grow rapidly, even without any major anti-aging medical breakthrough. In the UK, there are now more people of pensionable age than under 16. As economist George Magnus points out in *The Age of Aging*, this is a phenomenon already felt acutely in Japan, Germany and Italy and soon to affect most Western countries as well as the economic powerhouse of China. He points out that the median age of the world's population (where half the population are older and half are younger) will rise from 28 now to 38 by 2050. It will be 47 in Europe by that time, 45 in China and about 41 in North America and Asia.[18]

How can we provide for an aging population out of the taxation revenues from a shrinking younger generation? One answer is an increase in retirement ages, which is already happening. If people are fit to work into their 70s, then why should they expect to stop when they are 60 and live for 20–30 years on a combination of their savings and government support? This has been difficult to achieve in a world where work consists of full-time jobs, but new work styles will make the idea of gradual retirement both possible and normal.

Future work for all sectors

As we show throughout the book, leading employers have started to realize that modernizing their work practices is essential to running an effective organization. The high-tech sector started the trend, with some professional services firms following on, but we have found examples of future work leaders in many different industries and countries, and in both private and public sectors. Some sectors are more reluctant than others to embrace change, however. In the finance sector in particular, there is still an addiction to the long-hours culture, and some manufacturing companies think that new work styles do not apply to them. But as pioneers emerge in their industries, others will follow suit.

One global company in the consumer goods sector that has recently embarked on the shift to future work is **Unilever**. It launched an 'Agile Working' strategy at the end of 2009, driven by business objectives. 'Agile Working is a simple but powerful concept,' says Paul Polman, CEO of Unilever. 'It affords everyone at Unilever the opportunity to work with maximum flexibility and minimal constraints, enabled by technology and specially designed office facilities.' This increases productivity, reduces the need for travel and its associated costs and helps people to achieve greater balance in their lives, he adds.

The company has made the connection between business success and new ways of working. It has recognized that this is a way to increase the diversity of its leadership and get the best return from its human resources. And it understands that this involves a change in culture. We look at how Unilever is doing this at its futuristic new offices in Hamburg in Chapter 6 and we analyze the group's agile working strategy in Chapter 8.

New types of work contract

The last decade of the twentieth century brought a rapid growth in the flexibility of employment contracts. Part-time work, staggered hours, condensed working weeks and 'flexi-time' spread. Remote and home-based working increased with the introduction of mobile technologies. But these were mainly just variations of the permanent, full-time job.

The following decade saw an expansion of the 'contingent workforce'. Organizations kept hold of a core of essential talent but contracted out peripheral activities to save costs and increase flexibility. This paid off during the recession when many businesses shed temporary staff but managed to hold on to their permanent staff ready for the upturn. The trend toward a more flexible model of work has raised the question of whether organizations need to be burdened with liabilities for 'permanent' employees at all. Even in the public sector a permanent job offer is no longer necessarily a lifetime commitment.

The Internet has given birth to a new type of organization that can tap into the talent of individuals without taking over their lives. The network business, the virtual corporation and the e-enterprise are versions of this emerging entity. They contract with individuals to supply their services, but not through a conventional employment contract. They pull together collections of individual contributors to achieve a common aim. They are 'free agents' who can choose a lifestyle without the ties and constraints of conventional employment. The world they inhabit has much in common with the pre-industrial era. They are more likely to be working from home, some perhaps in a rural setting, and building social relationships in their home community rather than in the office. As work evolves into a new era, future generations may reflect back on the 200 years of Industrial Age working practices and see them as a passing phase in our social history.

Here are three examples of these new types of business:

Amplify Trading, the company for which the two Dutch men at the start of Chapter 1 worked for a while, shows how technology is changing parts of the financial industry. The London-based financial futures trading firm, which launched during the credit crunch in early 2009, trades on its own account as well as training graduates to become traders and analysts.

It all takes place through a virtual trading room, with traders and trainees logging in via their laptops from Australia, China, the US, Spain and other countries. 'The speed of the internet systems allows us to risk-manage our larger traders as if they were here in London,' says Will de Lucy, the firm's co-founder. 'We can share voice and text and charts and live video online. The amount of information is much greater than having 80 guys just shouting at each other on a traditional trading floor.'

The firm avoids the overheads of a trading floor in London and has access to talent around the world, while the traders have a lot of flexibility about when and where they work. Two recent trainees are young mothers trading from home. De Lucy says that a spin-off benefit of remote trading, especially for women, is 'not having to be involved in all the lads' banter on a typical trading floor which can put people off'.

Success is all about performance, in this case how much profit people make from their trades. There are no employment contracts. The firm's 35 proprietary traders are effectively self-employed, trading through Amplify's systems. The deal is that the firm covers their losses and receives 40 percent of their profits, but if they prove highly successful they may negotiate to keep a higher percentage. 'There's nothing to tie them to us, except that through this communications room they receive all the information and discussion that helps their performance,' says de Lucy.

Based in Santa Clara, California, **LiveOps** uses a dispersed workforce of around 20,000 independent agents, mostly working from their homes across the US, to provide virtual call center services on demand for businesses. The agents include a high proportion of women, as well as retired people and students, and many have caring responsibilities.

Pay depends on their performance and the volume of service they pro-vide. Some clients pay a simple rate, generally 25 cents per minute of talk time, some pay a base rate in addition to a bonus for commission and some pay entirely on commission.[19] Such 'e-lance' businesses are open to criti-cism over their pay rates and lack of employment rights, benefits and job security. However, LiveOps says that 'an average agent can make well over minimum wage' and points to the flexibility that freelance operators have.

Agents can choose where they work, although calls can only be routed to their regular business line, not re-routed if they are traveling. They can choose when to provide their services, which can be in blocks of just 30 minutes, and it is up to them whether to develop their skills or not.

Maynard Webb, chairman and CEO of LiveOps, argues that this work model does not replace existing models but creates opportunities for people who do not want to, or cannot, work in the traditional way. 'There is a huge need just for a solution for part-time remote work and we are pleased to be solving this today.'[20]

With a large dispersed and independent workforce, Webb says it is nec-essary to find ways of building 'a self-sustaining community'. 'We provide our contract workforce with access to resources to interact as a community, motivate each other and self-regulate their own businesses' performance.' There is a LiveOps University, which runs e-learning programs, and there are discussion groups on topics such as building a successful business and creating performance-based goals.

Despite past proposals for legislative changes that would make it more difficult for such companies to rely on an army of independent contractors rather than employees, LiveOps told us its business model was not under threat. In March 2011, it announced a partnership with the city of Newark, New Jersey, to create new work opportunities and said it was looking at similar partnerships with other US cities and states.

At what might be considered the other end of the work scale, **Eden McCallum** is a UK-based management consulting firm that draws on a pool of 400 independent consultants and matches them to clients' projects, but does not employ them directly. Launched in 2000, it has attracted highly qualified professionals who want more control over their working lives while maintaining their earning power. About half the consultants previ-ously worked for big firms such as McKinsey, Bain and Boston Consulting Group.

As founding director Liann Eden explains, strong interpersonal skills are as important as ever in managing the consultants, even though this network model is based on looser affiliations than the traditional employer–employee contract. They still need feedback, reinforcement and a sense of belonging. 'Being very clear in our communications is very important in this network model,' she says. 'We've got very good at setting clear expectations about the frequency and nature of the work up front. They know exactly where they stand. They know our standards.'

To ensure effective communication, the firm uses a contact management system that records every contact with each consultant, every project they have done and every client they have worked with. It also captures all the information about and feedback on the consultant from interviews, references and project debriefs. This means that the in-house team can interact knowledgably with the consultants, almost as if they were staff.

The firm also runs regular information and training events for the consultants to meet, exchange experiences and stay on top of developments. 'That's where they get a sense of identity,' says Charlotte Cameron, the partner leading the firm's consultant-focused activities. 'People say it's great to feel part of something. We also get consultants together to tell them what we're planning for the future of the firm. It's about sharing information with them so that we as an organization are not a black hole.'

Trust is a big part of the relationship, as the firm's founders discovered. After they launched in 2000, they were worried that some of their growing pool of consultants might bypass them and seek work directly from their client companies or vice versa. They required them to sign a contract saying they could approach the clients only through Eden McCallum. 'Two to three years in, we realized that the consultants and clients aren't interested in one-off transactions,' says Eden. 'The consultants want to work with us as a conduit to lots of interesting clients and projects. Clients want to work with us to solve many different issues, not just what one consultant can do. Over the past 10 years we've done over 1000 projects and I can count on one hand the number of times someone tried to go behind our backs.'[21]

In summary

We are on the cusp of the next big transformation in the model of work. Today technology allows us to work very differently than we did even a decade ago, and the new generation joining the workforce is not the only one demanding a new deal. Demographic and social trends, particularly the changing role of women, all point to the need for a fresh approach to work. We are poised for a revolution in working practices.

In Chapter 3 we show how future work will emerge as a product of these changes, built on a model of individual autonomy and a culture of trust and responsibility.

CHAPTER 3

Turning convention on its head

Organizations that remove the artificial boundaries around how, where and when work gets done are those that are winning in today's marketplace. They are more flexible, more efficient, and better able to respond to rapid change.

Fiona Laird, co-lead, 'Agile Working' program, Unilever

Which of the following two companies sounds more like yours?

Company 1 offers its employees a range of 'flexible work arrangements'. Reduced hours, flexible start and finish times and compressed weeks (four ten-hour days instead of five eight-hour days) are all available. The HR department encourages individuals to talk about their personal situation so that the management and the individual can find a response that suits both. Employees can have paid time off for personal needs and can take it in one-hour slots, for example to attend a school event or have a longer lunch. Chair massages are available when peak work demands push up the stress levels. 'Our employees tell us how grateful they are that we offer these arrangements,' says the head of HR.

Company 2 has invested in laptops, handheld devices and internet-based phone systems so that all employees can access work databases from anywhere. By encouraging remote working, it has retained talented people who have moved to the other side of the world and, in some cases, gained new business through them. It has abolished the traditional definition of paid time off. People can take any number of days' break, provided they meet their objectives and customers' requirements. Everyone on the staff, from senior professionals to junior assistants, is able to arrange their work around other priorities such as family care, volunteer work, or training and development. The company says that this kind of flexibility is a business survival tool.

We suspect that, if you are a lucky Westerner, you probably work for an organization like Company 1. However, we will show in this chapter why Company 1's approach involves only a small tinkering at the edges, and no fundamental change to the standard work model that we have described as outmoded and unsuited to the twenty-first century. Company 2, on the other hand, represents the future, because it has made the essential shift from controlling and measuring the time people spend at work to measuring and rewarding people based on how well they perform and what results they produce.

There is a wide spectrum of jobs in the world today and both these examples are at one end. They both attempt to provide an environment in which employees will be motivated to perform. Although their approaches are very different, they are built on the assumption that caring about people is a good business investment.

Sadly, there are still many employers around the world that appear not to care much about their employees' motivation or welfare. They treat people as disposable assets that are simply units of production in a business process, expecting them to clock up excessively long hours, often doing repetitive, mind-numbing work.

From time to time, when things go badly wrong, labor conditions in the factories churning out goods for Western consumers make the headlines. Such was the case in 2010, when a spate of worker suicides put the spotlight on Foxconn, which makes electronic devices in China for big brands including Apple, Dell, Nokia and Sony. The company employs an army of 300,000 people at its Shenzhen factory city, where workers sleep in company dormitories and work long hours of overtime under a management regime which would be unacceptable in the West.

With such well-known corporate customers, the suicides at Foxconn were big news. Leading brands have supplier codes of conduct which specify a level of dignity and respect for workers. They carry out audits of supplier facilities. Apple's chief operating officer and other executives went to China to investigate. After the suicides, Foxconn raised wages and put an employee assistance program in place. Apple's 2011 progress report said Foxconn had 'begun the process of expanding operations to other parts of China, enabling workers to be closer to their home provinces'.[1] This is part of a wider shift of production by companies to inland China, which is being driven by the rise in labor costs in the big coastal manufacturing hubs.[2]

Compared with such labor issues in emerging markets, the stresses involved in high-powered jobs in Western multinationals might pale into insignificance. But they do have some common features. In both cases, people are expected to sacrifice their personal lives for the good of the company and work in often highly pressurized environments. For some, the high rewards and challenges make this acceptable. But others burn out, or quit for a saner life.

As one executive who left his job with a global technology group told us: 'When the expectation is to be available 24×7 *and* be at the office each day for no productive reason, then insanity occurs.'

His team, who had to support internal customers in other time zones, had been used to working from home because their job involved long hours, primarily late at night. Then the new boss above him decreed that they should also commute into the office during the business day. 'When it became a requirement for employees to sit at the office during business hours for the sake of being there, many felt completely defeated. The "flexible" work environment was not so much a way for employees to work more effectively and with more flexibility, but as a way for the company to extract every extra bit of productivity out of each employee without having to pay for it.'

The trouble with flexible working

Flexible working has been around for 40 years in various forms. It started with 'flexi-time', which gave people the opportunity to vary their hours within strictly limited boundaries. Employers defined the 'core hours' and then allowed some choice outside those times, such as a two-hour window for people to vary their arrival and departure times.

These schemes allowed employees to fit in other commitments at the beginning and end of the working day but were problematic for managers because people could change their flexi hours on a day-to-day basis and 'bank' hours to take as extra days' holiday. Meetings had to be restricted to core hours or negotiated with employees weeks in advance.

Flexi-time schemes can also undermine productivity because people are more likely to stop work when their paid time is finished if they are recording their hours and 'clocking in and out'. So this form of flexible time is going out of fashion and being replaced with something more predictable and less likely to lead to clock-watching, such as 'compressed hours'.

A common example of compressed hours is the 'nine day fortnight' where each working day is lengthened slightly and by the end of nine days the employee has worked the equivalent of ten. This is usually a fixed pattern, so is more predictable than flexi-time, but brings its own difficulties. Friday is by far the most popular day for people to choose as their 'day off', which is not a problem until the demand cannot be met. Then Fridays off have to be rationed.

Today, if an organization employs people on any contract other than the conventional one, whether it is part time, job sharing, term-time work and so on, it is likely to be labeled 'flexible working'.

However, these various flexible hours options simply shift the time that the work is performed. People are still expected to work for a set number of hours per week or month and are paid accordingly. Part-time workers are paid pro rata, and job sharers are paid their share based on the split in time, even though, in practice, they are often more productive than one full-time person. Home workers frequently have to log in to a time-management system to count their hours. Flexible time has been pasted on to conventional fixed work patterns without any fundamental change in the work model, but with a lot more complexity.

The second key variable in flexible working is location. The choice of where we work has opened up over the last decade with mobile technology. There is remote working, location-independent working, home working and other variations on the theme. People work on the move, with their BlackBerrys, iPads, netbooks and smartphones. But again, this is often on top of conventional work.

So employees work their eight-hour day at their desk, then are expected to use technology to extend the day, take work home or keep in touch while they are traveling. Work has invaded personal space, instead of helping to free people's time.

The scourge of the 'long-hours culture'

International business executives who operate in a time zone different from the headquarters country often experience some of the most extreme demands of all. Take the case of Katrin, a highly experienced senior executive based in Europe working for a US multinational, who had to travel two or three weeks in every month between continents as her responsibilities grew. She hardly saw her children. When she was back at base in Europe, she regularly had to take part in teleconferences at 8 p.m. or 9 p.m. to accommodate the US team, thus missing dinner with the family, and then her inbox would be full of 'urgent' emails first thing in the morning. Exhausted and demoralized, she was eventually diagnosed with burnout. She quit for a senior job at another large company that gave her back control over her schedule and her life.[3]

The long-hours culture often goes hand in hand with 'presenteeism', where people feel they have to be in the office regardless of whether they have something productive to do. If being seen to be working is a good thing, then being seen to be working for longer is better. Making sure your car is still in the car park when your boss leaves the office is a sound route to promotion. Hanging an extra coat on the back of the chair to show you are there, even if you have actually popped out for a sandwich, is extreme, but it happens.

It is hardly surprising that the long-hours culture has become ingrained in some sectors and countries such as the US and UK. People are often well rewarded for those extra hours. Some employees will be paid for every minute past their allotted time and, if this is deemed to be at 'antisocial' times, they will be paid a premium. So there is every incentive to slow down work during weekdays to ensure there is some left over for evenings and weekends. This is a sure recipe for low productivity.

The salaried employee may not be paid directly for the extra hours but their 'dedication' will still be noted and the reward will come eventually. As long as employers choose to reward effort and not results, long hours will persist.

Flexing time and place

So what is the solution? Turn convention on its head, as Company 2 did, moving away from defining work by time and location. Most 'knowledge work' today can be done completely independently of both time and location, while many other jobs are much more restricted by one or the other, or both. Yet even these jobs can often be fundamentally rethought, drawing on the knowledge of those at the front line, as we will show.

A wide spectrum of working styles can co-exist within a single organization, as demonstrated at **Vodafone UK**'s modern headquarters outside Newbury, west of London. At one end are the mobile teams, such as sales staff, who are out most of the time but in the office for team meetings once a week. Mid-way along are the staff who are based in the office but who can work remotely; when they are there, they pick a free desk, or meet at a table in the canteen, and their hours are not monitored. At the other end is the network operations center, which has to run with military precision 24 hours a day, 365 days a year. Everyone here is dressed in uniform black, a stark contrast with the casual dress code elsewhere in the building. Center staff have no choice over the location of their work, but they have a degree of flexibility over timing: they work in shifts that are self-rostered, with management guidance when needed.

Looking at jobs in terms of their dependence on time and place gives a clear picture of the options available for new ways of working. **Figure 3.1** shows four quadrants representing the options, as depicted in a report by Britain's Equal Opportunities Commission (now part of the Equality and Human Rights Commission).[4]

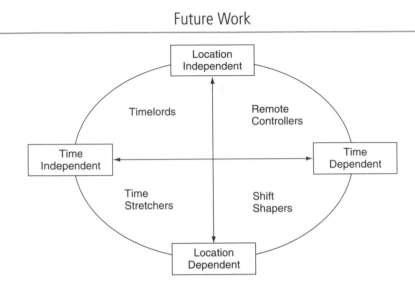

Figure 3.1 Categories of workers

It shows that even people who are unable to vary the hours or location of work can still have some flexibility in their choice of shift. Hence they are categorized as 'Shift-shapers'. Examples are health care workers and police officers who have to be in fixed places for much of their work but who also have tasks such as planning and administration that could be done at home or in another location.

People with flexibility over both time and place are described as 'Timelords'. Those with some flexibility in time but with a static location for their work are 'Time-stretchers', and those with fixed times but variable locations are 'Remote-controllers'.

The Commission mapped all 353 occupations in the UK government's standard classification of jobs on to this diagram and estimated that about 60 percent of workers were in the occupations in the bottom right of the chart, where time and location flexibility are traditionally less available.

Describing this category, the report says it contains slightly more women (around 55 percent) than men. 'Within it, though, there are significant gender differences with men being more concentrated in occupations where the production process is thought to restrict flexibility (eg. assemblers, vehicles and metal goods). About six in ten of those in these types of occupations are men.

'Women are more concentrated in front line occupations where the daily flow of customer demand is thought to restrict flexibility (eg. check-out operators). Around seven in ten of those in these types of occupation are

women. But in both cases, despite the business realities of these occupations, models are possible that increase the degree of flexibility so that
people gain some control over their work.'

It points out that about 45 percent of these people are in the bottom quar-
tile of jobs, typically the lowest paid, and often have the least control over
their working lives. This can be detrimental 'not only for the wellbeing
and aspirations of employees, but also for the commitment and productivity
from which employers can potentially gain'.

The Commission found that one in seven employees fitted the Timelords
category, people who have substantial control over when and where they
work. Men account for six out of ten employees in these occupations and
around three-fifths of the occupations in this quadrant are in the top-quartile,
highest paying jobs. So, varying a combination of time and place of work
can be the most rewarding pattern for employee as well as employer. This
is because it gives autonomy to the individual while boosting productivity
for the employer.

Up until relatively recently, most work had to be performed at the
employer's premises, and this happened under the watchful eye of a super-
visor or manager. If employees were at their workstation, they were deemed
to be working. Where the job was part of a production line, this made some
sense. But it has little relevance to today's knowledge work.

If someone is sitting at a desk, or in a meeting, there is no guarantee they
are working productively. Yet their employment contract almost certainly
does not mention productivity. It defines the hours they are expected to work
and the compensation they will receive. If they turn up for work and are busy
doing something that appears to be useful, they are paid at the end of the
month.

Today's low productivity model is ready for reform. Tomorrow's model
is a high productivity work process that gives better satisfaction to the
individual and the manager. It supports the organization's goals, improves
output and gives employees more manageable lives, all at once. That is what
'future work' is about.

Future work

Future work is based on the simple principle that work is an activity that
produces a desired result. It is performed to achieve outcomes which contribute to the enterprise that has engaged the worker, whether as employee
or contractor.

The tasks carried out in the name of 'work' are useless if they have no
detectable output. Yet many organizations have lost sight of this. Managers

turn business requirements into a job description and person specification, run it through the job evaluation system and recruit someone who appears to meet the criteria. They pay for the time of the employee at a rate calculated according to the skills needed for the job. Somewhere in this process, the direct relationship between work and output gets lost.

A new approach is emerging to challenge this. It is called results-based working and is a core element of future work. It challenges[6] convention by asking the following questions:

- Instead of paying for inputs, regardless of their usefulness, why not pay for outputs?
- Instead of rewarding long hours of low productivity, why not reward shorter hours of high productivity?
- Instead of encouraging people to be seen at the workplace at defined times, why not encourage people to work where and when they are most productive?

Getting results

Measuring results in itself is not new. 'Management by objectives' was a management fad in the 1960s. Most organizations have a performance appraisal system and many have bonus schemes based on achieving targets.

What is new is the introduction of systems that just look at results and ignore other traditional management constraints. So the amount of time you put into achieving the result is irrelevant; it is what you achieve that counts. Where and when you do the work does not matter; producing the output to the right quality and on time does.

Some innovative and successful Fortune 500 companies have embraced this model as an essential business strategy, say consultants Tom Harnish and Kate Lister in their report, *Results Based Management*.[5] 'They've learned that when they ignore the where, when, and how work is done, and focus on results, their people are more productive, more creative, and more successful.' They also argue that this new way of working allows companies to do more with less – fewer buildings, less pollution, less overtime and less waste. Their employees are doing more with less too – fewer distractions, less stress and less commuting. 'For companies, that all translates into greater loyalty, engagement, and productivity.'

One such system is the Results-Only Work Environment, known as ROWE[SM]. This is described in detail in *Why Work Sucks*[6] by Cali Ressler and Jody Thompson, who introduced the approach at **Best Buy**, the

US consumer electronics company. It started in a small way in 2001 as a move to make the company an employer of choice. In 2003, it was named ROWE and, based on its success, spread across the corporate staff so that, by 2008, 80 percent were in the scheme.

Senior management were impressed with the results and Brad Anderson, Best Buy's CEO, was supportive, agreeing to let Ressler and Thompson promote ROWE outside the company. This became the real testing ground for the results-only concept. It may have worked in a progressive company like Best Buy but would it work elsewhere? Five years later, at least 13 companies have officially completed the ROWE migration process and many more have been experimenting with the system.

In March 2010, President Obama announced that the Office of Personnel Management would pilot a ROWE program, with the intent of rolling it out to the rest of the federal government if successful. The retailer Gap has adopted ROWE in its Outlet division and halved employee turnover as a result (see Chapter 8 for the full Gap story).

ROWE successfully disconnected the value of someone's work from the effort that they put in. There is, therefore, no pressure on people to turn up to work, attend meetings and impress the boss with long hours of dedicated effort. As long as they achieve the required results, employees have the freedom to work any way they want. They are also encouraged to challenge established practices. If they do not think a meeting is useful, then they do not need to attend. 'Every meeting is optional' is one of the guideposts laid down in the scheme. 'There is no judgment about how you spend your time' is another.

It's all about culture

However, the real success of future work is not in a set of rules about results-based working, it is in the change in culture of the organization and the way managers treat people as a result. Just introducing a results measurement system into a conventional management culture is unlikely to have much impact. In fact, there is likely to be a negative reaction from managers.

A pure results-only system relies on a relationship of trust between a manager and employee. It is based on the belief that when people are given a clear goal to achieve in a supportive environment, they will be motivated to do so without having to be monitored, supervised or forced. It assumes that most people will make good use of the freedom to manage their own work. They will choose to get things done in the way that best suits them and is most productive. They will want to achieve the best results, but in the shortest time practical, rewarding themselves with the extra time to use as they wish. This is the opposite of the usual 'pay for hours worked', which encourages and rewards long hours.

Successful U-turn for tax firm

In 2008, Ryan, a leading tax services firm in the US, decided to 'do a 180', and abandoned the approach it had taken to managing employees for almost 20 years. It moved from a face-time company to one that focuses on results.

Employees who were accustomed to rigid office hours and little flexibility found getting used to the 'myRyan' environment a challenge. 'It is easier said than done, and we knew it when we made the change,' says Delta Emerson, chief organizational development officer at Ryan.

The reason it made the U-turn was that it was experiencing higher staff turnover than it wanted, and the 'balance' word kept coming up in exit interviews. 'We were determined to find a way to continue to get the results that have made us so successful, but to tweak how we get there in a way that empowers our employees to have control over both their personal and professional lives.'

The scheme has dramatically reduced turnover, says Emerson. The key to focusing on results was having the ability to measure them, and not just in terms of the financial balance sheet. Individual 'dashboards' allow employees and the firm to monitor everyone's contributions to the bottom line, and their personal goals. 'We have put blood, sweat, and tears into creating this sophisticated scorecard that tracks individual progress and accomplishments toward achieving agreed-upon, quantifiable goals,' says Emerson. 'Everyone has access to their dashboard and has complete control over taking whatever steps are needed to stay on track.'

Ryan now allows employees to work anywhere, anytime, as long as the work gets done. Every employee has the freedom to set his or her own hours, and all employees have the technical resources needed to handle their jobs remotely. 'Bottom line, our firm is proof that any company can make this move successfully, if they sincerely want to, and if they do the work necessary to prepare the environment, resources, and processes.'[7]

Putting theory into practice

To progress beyond 'flexible' working to future work requires a fundamental review of the role of management. Managers need to understand how people are motivated and how to get the best out of them. To do this they need to put into practice lessons about motivation that have been around for the last 50 years. It helps to take a fresh look at how a few outstanding businesses have been getting 20–30 percent improvements in output from their people and ask why this is not happening everywhere.

In 1960, Douglas McGregor posed a key question to managers: What are your assumptions (implicit as well as explicit) about the most effective way to manage people?[8] His own answer was that there were two models, which he named 'Theory X and Theory Y'. Summarized simply, Theory X assumes that people have to be forced to work by constant management control while Theory Y contends that people are self-motivated and can be left to manage themselves.

Many more recent management gurus, such as Warren Bennis and Peter Drucker, have been influenced by McGregor's work. But his ideas are not just theoretical. They have been put into practice with positive effect by inspired CEOs who have recognized that traditional management is heavily 'Theory X' while their own beliefs about people are firmly 'Theory Y'.

In 1958, Bill Gore set up **W L Gore & Associates**, the company that makes Gore-Tex, the material used in many applications from outdoor clothing to artificial arteries. He established a structure and culture based on communication and cooperation rather than authority and hierarchy. Any person was allowed to make a decision as long as it was fair, encouraged others and made a commitment to the company.

Consultation was required only for decisions that could potentially cause serious damage to the enterprise. Furthermore, new associates joined the company on the same effective authority level as all the other workers, including Gore himself. There were no titles or bosses, with only a few exceptions, and commands were replaced by personal commitments.

This flat 'lattice' organization, which still tries to limit units to about 150 people, has stood the test of time. Not only has W L Gore been outstandingly successful financially, it still ranks highly among employees, appearing consistently near the top of the charts of the best employers. The reputation of the company has spread far and wide. It has been studied and admired by leaders of other organizations. Yet very few have been able to replicate the success. Why is this?

The challenge that proves insurmountable for most of those trying to emulate W L Gore is to remove the hierarchical structure and thinking in the organization. If managers see their role as directing employees, the Gore system won't work. It relies on a genuine belief that people are self-motivated and that by being empowered to control their own work they will flourish and produce great results.

But to put this into practice takes away managers' power to make decisions, delegate work and exercise their authority. It also strips them of the physical trappings of power and status. These are hurdles that are now being tackled by leaders in a range of other companies, and we will see in Chapters 5 and 6 how they are breaking through the barriers of 'macho management'.

W L Gore & Associates is so called because the people who work there are treated as associates who collaborate to achieve the company goals. There are no salary bands. It is rare for a manager to be recruited from outside, apparently because of the difficulty they would have in adjusting. Associates rank each other in annual surveys and earn the right to manage others based on the abilities they have demonstrated to their peers.[9]

Bill Gore also introduced 'dabble time' – half an hour each week which associates could spend as they wished as long as they were still meeting their main commitments. A few other organizations have versions of this scheme. **Google** allows its engineers to take 20 percent of their time to work on their pet projects, provided they can enlist a team of colleagues to collaborate.

A matter of motivation

Our proposals for future work are built on the principles laid down in McGregor's Theory Y and repeated in varying forms over the last half century by motivation theorists and management professors. The idea that people will respond willingly to being trusted and treated as adults fits in with Herzberg's motivation theory, Maslow's hierarchy of needs and the views of leading management thinkers of the late twentieth century, from Peter Drucker to Charles Handy, from Tom Peters to Gary Hamel. Empower your employees and you will reap the reward. If you believe people will react responsibly to being given freedom, don't just talk about Theory Y as a theory, manage as if you mean it.

Hamel states this succinctly in *The Future of Management*.[10] 'To a large extent, managers play the role of parents, school principals, crossing guards and hall monitors,' he says. 'They employ control from without because employees have been deprived of the ability to exercise control from within. Adolescents outgrow most of these constraining influences; employees often aren't given that chance. The result: disaffection. Adults enjoy being treated like 13-year olds even less than 13-year olds.'

Why do managers persist in treating people like children? The command model of management appears to be blind to the evidence that ranges from academic research to highly successful employers. Assume people are responsible, give them the freedom to manage themselves, treat them like adults and watch them flourish.

Hundreds of research papers point to the same conclusion. 'Human beings have an innate inner drive to be autonomous, self-determined, and connected to one another. And when that drive is liberated, people achieve more and live richer lives.' So says Daniel Pink in *Drive*[11], his excellent review of the theory and practice of motivation. He questions how much real autonomy people have under today's management practices. We may talk about 'empowerment' and 'flexibility' but current management still revolves around control. 'This era doesn't call for better management,' Pink says. 'It calls for a renaissance of self-direction.'

The epitome of self-direction is self-employment. Running yourself as an enterprise and charging your customers for your services means deciding for yourself how best to do the work. Many managers will happily engage a consultant or subcontract work to an individual without worrying about the working hours involved. They will leave the individual to do the work their own way and pay for the results when they are delivered. If this can be achieved with the self-employed, then why not engage employees on a results-only basis? In both cases, they are delivering a product through a self-managed process.

Autonomy at work

The best indicator of true autonomy at work is control of time and place. In a future work organization, the control is with employees as far as possible. They choose how to get the job done in the best way. They make informed, intelligent decisions because they are trusted to do so. They know what results they need to achieve and are motivated by the intrinsic satisfaction of doing a good job. If the job allows, they decide if and when they need to go to the employer's premises to get work done. They work when they are at their most productive, not just when their manager wants to see them. The results of our survey (covered in detail in Chapter 7) show that organizations moving toward future work are most likely to have a culture of trust and empowerment.

Most work can be expressed in the form of results, but as we showed above there are still many jobs that have to be done at a fixed time and/or place. So results-based systems will not replace conventional employment contracts where jobs necessitate working at specific times. However, what is done within those times can still be measured and rewarded on output as part of the mix of compensation.

Employees with limited choice of time and place of work may be involved in customer service that has to be provided in person or they may be part of a continuous process that needs to be operated at all times. The delivery of care to the elderly or nursing of the sick cannot be done remotely or at a time totally at the discretion of the employee. Yet in the UK, the National Health Service gives autonomy to groups of nurses to organize their own shift times and NHS Direct, a telephone help service, answers five million phone calls a year and employs 1400 trained nurses working remotely from their patients. A joint US–UK study of over 1700 patient care cases estimated that 45 percent of US patient care could be handled by telephone diagnosis and advice, or 'telemedicine'.[12]

A well-documented example of real autonomy is **Semco** in Brazil. In his best-selling book, *Maverick*,[13] Ricardo Semler explains how he took over the business from his father and totally changed the company culture. He abolished organization charts, job titles and trappings of power. He empowered employees to recruit their peers and their managers. He gave his workers as much freedom as possible, with influence on every decision the company made, from how the plants should look and where each section should be positioned to letting them set their own working hours and schedules as well as their pay.

In creating a real democracy with power resting with the employees, Semler would stand out as a brave and inspired leader in any environment. Managing to do this in Brazil at a time of economic chaos and destructive labor relations in the 1990s makes it more remarkable. Semco, which has survived through Brazil's economic downs and ups, has been used as an example of inspired leadership across the world, but very few organizations have been able to match the radical approach of Ricardo Semler. And many have indeed viewed him as a 'maverick'.

This approach to running an organization is seen as a threat. What is left for managers to do if employees are allowed to get on with the job under their own steam? How does the boss exercise authority if employees are coming and going whenever they choose? Those are the fears. In fact, we think managers still have a very important role to play, but it is different from the one that prevailed in the Industrial Age working model.

Happy Computers is a UK training company that has won a stack of workplace awards. Its visionary founder and CEO, Henry Stewart, has written a nine-point manifesto for a great workplace, including 'Give freedom within clear guidelines' and 'Select managers who are good at managing'. The latter is a simple principle, often ignored. 'Make sure your people are supported by somebody who is good at doing that, and find other routes for those whose strengths are elsewhere,' Stewart says. 'Even better, allow people to choose their managers.'[14]

Managing in a future work environment is about supporting people and enabling them to perform to maximum effectiveness. It is not telling people what to do, but helping them to see what is needed. It is about sharing goals and inspiring people to achieve them. It is about listening to employees and using their ideas and energy, not telling them to do what they are told. It is about trusting people to make their own decisions about how they get the job done, not watching their every move. It is about enabling them to work anytime, anywhere, as far as possible.

It is also about adapting work to the new majority workforce, for whom the old model does not fit, as we showed in Chapter 2. The restrictions of 'part-time' work, compressed hours or other flexible work arrangements currently hold back people's career progression and access to leadership roles, even though working this way is usually at least as productive, and often more so. Switching to the Company 2 model described at the start of this chapter renders categories such as 'full-time' and 'part-time' irrelevant.

As this new model spreads, it will become easier for both women and men to fit work around personal responsibilities and to have better access to leadership roles without being saddled with career-limiting labels.

In summary

It may take a new generation of managers to make future work a common reality. Companies such as W L Gore and Semco have benefited from enlightened CEOs whose values are reflected in every management action in the business. Others such as Ryan have changed their working practices through a fundamental shift in their management culture.

Now, however, the technological tools are available for every business to make this shift too. To do so successfully, managers must question their own assumptions about the most effective way to manage people. If they expect their employees to be present for fixed hours to prove they are working, is this because the work really requires it or because they do not trust their people with more freedom? Assuming that people will abuse the freedom if you give them a choice of working pattern is Theory X thinking.

Future work is based on Theory Y assumptions. Given freedom and responsibility, people will not abuse it. They will be at their most effective when they are self-motivated. They will get pleasure from doing a job well. Allowing them to define when and where they do their work is a tangible indicator that they have some autonomy. Managing people by results and not counting hours is another sign. The smart manager honestly answers McGregor's question and compares practice with principle. Belief in Theory Y is not enough. Implementing it involves a brave step from a manager: letting go of the reins and allowing people to flourish.

It's a big help in getting future work off the ground if you have a complete grasp of the business benefits. In Chapter 4 we will examine how some organizations have achieved great results by changing the way they manage their people. They have provided an autonomous working environment and trusted their staff to manage themselves. In return for their faith in their employees they have seen dramatic improvements in performance. Your organization could be next.

CHAPTER 4

Why it makes business sense

Workplace flexibility . . . affects the well-being of our families and the success of our businesses. It affects the strength of our economy – whether we'll create the workplaces and jobs of the future we need to compete in today's global economy.

President Barack Obama[1]

President Obama hosted a Workplace Flexibility Forum at the White House in 2010, bringing together CEOs, small business owners, labor leaders, policy experts and government officials. His message was that modernizing work is not just socially desirable but also good for business. He talked about why it mattered to the federal government as an employer.

'It's about attracting and retaining top talent in the federal workforce and empowering them to do their jobs, and judging their success by the results that they get – not by how many meetings they attend, or how much face-time they log, or how many hours are spent on airplanes,' he said.

How exactly does future work make sense for business? Here's how.

When **BDO USA**, the accounting firm, moved its New York office from Madison Avenue to Park Avenue, it was able to cut the space per person by 20 percent and achieve projected cost savings of $1.5m to $2m a year by encouraging teleworking. Not bad for a prime spot in Manhattan where office rents can be more than $100 per square foot.

In the UK, the supermarket chain **Sainsbury's** recorded a 65 percent jump in bread sales at a major London store after it involved its bakery staff in working out a schedule to meet customer demand for fresh bread throughout the day instead of only first thing in the morning.

Leading US insurance company **Chubb** halved the number of complaint calls, and extended the time employees were available to customers, when it asked teams to devise their own working patterns to meet targets for improved performance.

How have these three very different businesses done it? By handing people greater autonomy over how they work and how they achieve their business objectives.

In the case of BDO, the big reduction in office space is the result of a US-wide 'Flex Strategy' that encourages work practices such as telecommuting as a way to 'do more with less'. The firm gives people a large degree of control over where and when they work. Since this is a business strategy, not a human resources program, it measures the impact on the bottom line.

'Measuring was really important to show business leaders in the firm that it wasn't about being nice to employees but was essential to operating in the new world of global client demands,' says Marcee Harris Schwartz, director of the Flex Strategy.[2]

Sainsbury's scored its sales success at the Camden store in north London by the apparently simple, but often neglected, means of empowering front-line employees. Ziggie Singh, the store manager, invited the bakery team to devise a response to the change in shoppers' requirements. There was no flexibility about where they baked the bread, but there had to be flexibility about who did it at what time. Instead of imposing new working hours on them, as happens in many businesses, Singh asked them what *they* would do if they were in his shoes. The team came up with a system of rotating shifts that meant they could produce a regular supply of fresh bread while taking account of their varying personal and family commitments. 'It was more of a pull than a push style of management,' said Singh. 'Being involved in the whole process made the bakers more enthusiastic about the change.'[3]

Chubb did something similar with teams in various parts of the business across the US. The teams, who were jointly accountable with their managers for meeting the new business goals, worked collectively to find more efficient ways of doing their jobs that also accommodated their preferences, in this case for both working hours and location. Some started work earlier or finished later, thereby extending customer service cover; some opted to work from home several days a week to cut commuting time, while others chose to stick to a regular 8 a.m. to 5 p.m. office schedule, as a *Financial Times* article described.[4]

As well as the direct business outcomes – cost savings, increased sales, higher productivity – all three organizations reported a rise in employee satisfaction and motivation. So not only did the companies achieve improvements in financial performance, they also found that the approach they took to achieving these business goals had a direct and positive impact on how people felt about their jobs.

At Chubb, the business results from one such program involving 120 employees in the Chicago insurance claims department included: an increase from 90 percent to 100 percent in benefit payments made on time;

a rise in the percentage of customers contacted within 24 hours of making a claim; and productivity increases of at least 5 percent.

What's more, employees began to come up with more ideas for improving customer service and increasing market share. Here are some of their comments about the improvements they experienced:

'I feel less stressed and I am more focused on results'

'I am more excited to come to work and I feel my ideas are being heard'

'I can now put my kids on the bus'

'I see change as more positive, more opportunity'[5]

As we explained in Chapter 3, these approaches go beyond traditional flexible work arrangements, which are designed first and foremost as an accommodation to employees, and which tend to be granted only on request to certain individuals or groups. In traditional schemes, any positive outcomes tend to be ticks in the human resources box: greater staff loyalty; higher retention; lower absenteeism. While these are important, it is often difficult to measure the direct cause and effect. Not surprisingly, the link with the wider health and prosperity of the organization is often poorly understood.

Future work takes a more radical approach. It starts with business goals: to gain a competitive edge; to attract the best talent; to keep costs under control; to respond to rapid shifts in customer demand. It usually uses communications technology to make working practices more efficient and productive. It requires a culture of trust and empowerment, in which people are treated as adults and measured by results, not by the hours they work.

Cutting-edge companies are already demonstrating what this means for business. Companies that outperform their peers in terms of innovation and expansion into new markets are three times more likely to have adopted 'smarter working practices', according to an IBM survey of 275 senior executives around the world.[6] These practices include enabling people to stay connected by allowing them to work productively 'regardless of location, time or device'. In other words, giving them the tools and letting them get on with it.

By putting future work at the heart of the way the business operates, other organizations can also start to reap the performance gains that are demonstrated by the case studies in this chapter. Some of these gains have an immediate and tangible effect on the bottom line. Others emerge over the longer term and are harder to measure directly, but have the potential to make an even greater and more sustainable impact on a company's success.

To understand better the range of performance gains your business could experience from future work, we categorize them as tangible and intangible.

Tangible gains include:

- Higher productivity
- Improved customer service
- Resources better matched to customer demand
- Faster response to market changes
- Faster access to new markets
- Cost savings on real estate, utilities and services
- Cost savings on business travel
- Reduction in CO_2 emissions
- Lower staff sickness and absenteeism
- Lower staff turnover

Intangible gains include:

- Reduced risk of business disruption
- Greater customer loyalty
- Improved access to key contracts
- More creative output from employees
- Stronger management skills
- Higher employee morale and loyalty
- Lower management overheads due to employee self-management
- Healthier workforce, less prone to burnout
- Retention of knowledge and skills
- More transparent succession planning
- Access to wider sources of talent
- More women in senior management
- Enhanced employer reputation
- Contribution to environmental sustainability

It is tempting for finance directors to look at the tangible savings that can be made, particularly in real estate, and see future work as a cost-cutting exercise. Getting better use of buildings by more efficient use of space is a sensible business goal. It is easy to see and measure the savings when a building is vacated or a floor sub-let. But the real financial impact comes when the issue of productivity is addressed. For most organizations, getting 10 percent more output from their employees – or saving 10 percent on employee costs – would eclipse all the space savings they could possibly make.

By focusing on outputs, future work forces managers to value productivity. If they are going to reward people for their achievements, not their hours, then they need to measure these, as shown by the case studies in this chapter.

On top of these gains for individual organizations, more efficient working offers wider environmental and social benefits. By adopting future work, you can help to save the planet by reducing commuter and business car journeys and air travel, building and running smaller offices and thus cutting CO_2 emissions. There are huge long-term social benefits in having a healthier labor force that is better able to balance family and personal time with work requirements and that includes people who would otherwise be unable to do paid productive work because they have disabilities or are caring for children or elderly relatives.

We will now look at some of the business gains in detail, with examples from a range of organizations, large and small, private and public sector, which have already reaped the benefits.

Productivity gains

There is a large body of evidence that giving people autonomy over where and when they work tends to boost their output. This is partly because they have fewer distractions from office meetings and interruptions. People concentrate better if they can work at least some of the time in a quieter location, escape the stress of a long commute, or be freed of worries about how to manage both work and personal commitments. Trusted to get on with the job, people tend to be more motivated to do so, especially if they gain more time as a result. They may actually be working a few hours longer without realizing it, because work is more integrated into the rest of their lives.

Cisco, the leading international producer of networking equipment, might well be expected to record the business benefits it derives from remote working – and it does. Eighty-five percent of its employees telecommute and no one except call center operatives has a set work schedule. In a study of employees who use its 'Virtual Office' equipment to work from home for part of the week, they reported being nearly 50 percent more productive than in the office. The average employee using this equipment gained 2.75

productive work hours per week, which would typically have been spent commuting.[7]

These findings are remarkably similar to those of a productivity survey by the UK Telework Association. In this study, 85 percent of people who worked from home for at least part of each week reported an increase in how much they achieved. A quarter of those who were able to measure their output said they were over 50 percent more productive. Only 5 percent thought they were less productive at home.

The main reasons they gave for their higher productivity were fewer interruptions, the ability to fit work alongside other commitments and time saved on commuting, at least some of which was then devoted to work. A third of respondents also cited loyalty and repayment of trust as a reason for their improved productivity.[8]

In our own survey of 366 managers, covered in more detail in Chapter 7, 88 percent of the respondents agreed or strongly agreed with the statement 'I believe people are more productive given autonomy over their working patterns', and 84 percent said they believed new ways of working would benefit the business.

Likewise, in a national survey by Microsoft in the US in 2010, 71 percent of employees said they were more productive when they were working away from the office. Only 11 percent said they were less productive, while 18 percent thought their output was about the same in the office as away from it.[9]

Telework payback

The initial investment in technology to support a telework program produces a return of between 200 percent and 1500 percent, according to analysis by the US government's General Services Administration, the agency responsible for federal facilities. This return takes the form of increased productivity, reduced absenteeism, lower real estate costs and reduced recruitment and retention needs.

'Our experience is also backed up by a pilot (GSA) program that we recently ran out of our Kansas City office,' Martha Johnson, administrator of the GSA, said in a speech to the US Telework Exchange in October 2010. 'This 90-day project moved 42 employees to telework. Two-thirds of them had the option to telework five days per week. Our results were great. Seventy-seven per cent of participants reported that their productivity had increased. Sick leave went down 69 per cent, saving on average 14 hours of work time per employee. Peer-to-peer communication increased almost 55 per cent.' There was also a predicted reduction of 30 metric tons of CO_2 due to reduced commuting.

Johnson said that telework 'is best when an entire group does it together, when they are empowered by collaborative technologies, and when there is a "water cooler manager" who facilitates social networking. There needs to be a "just do it" attitude across the organization.' For more guidance on effective management techniques for future work, see Chapters 8 and 9.

Bringing it all back home

As part of its 'Work Smart' strategy, BT, the UK communications group, introduced 'homeshoring', cutting back on call center premises and moving the jobs to individual agents' homes. These home-based operators are up to 30 percent more productive than those based in physical contact centers partly because they can respond to the daily fluctuations in incoming calls, says Caroline Waters, director of people and policy.[10]

'We've always wanted, from a business perspective, to have split shifts because there are natural peaks and troughs in customers' needs,' she says. 'The peaks tend to be morning, at lunchtime when people are ordering things or ringing in and saying that something isn't working, and in the early evening when people are coming home. Employees aren't going to drive into work for part of the day, go back, and then come back in again later. But if they're at home they can productively use the troughs to do shopping, taking care of the kids or elderly relatives, or having essential health services such as kidney dialysis, or whatever they need to do, and then "return to" work when they are most needed.'

In the US, BT has introduced on–off shifts lasting 40 minutes for home-based 'call minders' for its teleconference services. These employees guide callers through the teleconference process. The shifts are long enough to cover a typical teleconference. They then take a break before the next shift. Waters says this is a helpful way to work for people with caring responsibilities, such as those looking after an elderly relative.

Higher productivity does not, however, depend exclusively on being able to work away from the office or spend time at home. Simply having greater autonomy over one's working day can boost efficiency.

A two-year study of formal and informal flexibility in seven large UK-based companies found that most flexible workers, as well as their colleagues and managers, rated the quality and quantity of their individual work as being as good as, or better than, when they had worked standard schedules. They were also more committed than their peers to their organization.

These employees worked a variety of patterns, from having control over their start and finish times, to occasional working from home, through to more formal reduced-hours arrangements. 'I probably wouldn't be doing this job if I couldn't do it the way I am,' said one respondent in the study by Cranfield School of Management and the charity Working Families.[11] 'I would probably have left the company.'

Another interviewee highlighted the efficiency gains from rethinking how work is done. 'I started focusing on only going to the meetings where I could get something out of it, or the company would get something out of it,' she said.

Cost savings

Companies have to control costs during economic upswings as well as downturns. However, the global financial and economic crisis that began in 2007 has put a particularly severe squeeze on costs, even in the most financially robust companies, and led to massive cuts in both public and private sector jobs and services in many economies around the world.

For managers anxiously seeking ways to do more with less, future work provides two important solutions: it can reduce the amount spent on fixed costs such as office premises, and it can lower spending on recruitment, training and emergency cover by reducing staff turnover and absenteeism.

Efficiencies on office space are achievable both immediately and over the longer term, and they can be substantial. **IBM**, a pioneer of new working practices driven by business need, says it saves more than $100m a year on office space by operating a highly flexible, mobile workforce.

Seventy percent of the technology company's 400,000 employees work from home at least once a week. About 40 percent are classified as 'mobile', which means they have no fixed office and either work at home, at client sites, in airport lounges and trains, or at hot desks in IBM locations. The ratio of office space to employee is now 8:1, with some facilities as high as 15:1.[12]

BT calculates that it has reduced its office costs by more than £500m since 2000. It has realized ongoing annual savings of more than £50m a year by adopting mobile and home working over the past 20 years. Over 75 percent of its 79,000 people in the UK have flexible schedules. 'We have about 10,500 home-based workers and they save us £6000 a year each in office accommodation costs,' says Caroline Waters. 'Adding it all up, savings plus additional productive time, has created business value of over £70m a year.'

The freed-up space in BT's 1960s headquarters building near St Paul's Cathedral in London has been turned over to new activities. The basement now houses a large auditorium, a film studio and editing suite, an area to showcase new technology and a 'touchdown' zone for visiting staff. This innovative use of space saves costs, while the ability to demonstrate new products and services generates revenues. Referring to the auditorium, for example, Waters says: 'It could cost £15,000 a day to hire a space like this in London.'

Local government efficiencies

Faced with the need to reduce costs and vacate their main building, **Hinckley & Bosworth Borough Council**, a local authority in the English Midlands, decided to review their working practices and challenge some inbuilt assumptions.

Starting with the 30 or so staff in the Revenues and Benefits section, who were keen to participate, they introduced a variety of new working options in 2010. About 200 people now use remote access facilities to be able to work away from the office, from home or other locations. About 100 employees now have flexible contracts, some varying their hours, some working remotely, which has saved the authority £80,000 a year through efficiency.

Sanjiv Kohli, deputy chief executive (corporate direction), says this has happened at a time of significantly increased demand for housing benefits, and while some employees have been away on maternity leave. 'Historically we would have taken on agency staff to cover but this time we didn't need to,' he says. 'We've increased the throughput of new claims by three per day for each claims assessor. If you ask them how this has happened they will say it's because of flexible working.'

The Council will save up to £1m per year in accommodation and about £200,000 a year in employee costs, including reduced absenteeism and employee turnover, plus reduced use of temporary staff. The council has reduced headcount by the equivalent of 23 full-time employees while maintaining the level of service to the public, he says. There will be further efficiency savings in the future through improved flexible work practices.

'It's not easy but the benefits are worth it. We took a team that were keen to do it and supported them. They reported back the benefits and made it look so attractive that others wanted to follow,' adds Kohli. 'Our view is that how you manage remote people should be absolutely no different than managing people in the office. Just because you can see people doesn't mean you know they are working.'

If people want to work from home, they are expected to do it for at least 40 percent of the time and give up the right to a desk of their own in the office. Of those who have tried this, three decided they were too lonely working at home but the rest are thriving with improved work–life balance and increased productivity.

Improved customer response

Giving people autonomy and responsibility to make decisions without constantly having to refer upward can accelerate the business process. It can enable a faster response to customer needs, as BDO USA found when it wanted to move into new territory (see case study at the end of this chapter). In rapidly shifting markets, reacting quickly can be critical, as Guy Laurence, head of **Vodafone UK**, explains when talking about the open environment in which employees, including the directors, work, with no private offices, no personal desks and virtually no paper. 'The way to operate faster as a company is to move to this way of working rather than in a traditional closed office environment,' he says. 'The time to market is a prerequisite of success. As a consequence, companies have got to speed up. It used to take us 90 days to change a price plan. Now we do it in four days.'[13]

When teams are given the opportunity to work out their own schedules to suit their personal needs and those of the business, a common result is an extension of 'opening hours' or customer service cover. This is what **Chubb** found in the example at the start of this chapter. There were unexpected benefits as well: people learned how to do each other's roles so that they could cover for them when they were not in the office. They also took more initiatives themselves to ensure customer service, and jumped in if there was an unexpected absence.

Business continuity

Terrorist attacks, influenza pandemics and natural disasters all threaten serious disruptions to business. Official advice suggests that large organizations should plan for an extra 15 percent of staff being absent at the peak of a flu pandemic, and that small businesses should plan for 30 percent absence.[14] Businesses are regularly exhorted to draw up contingency plans for this and other types of disruption, such as Iceland's volcanic ash cloud that shut down big sections of European airspace during the spring of 2010. In these circumstances, efficient future work practices help to keep businesses going.

One investment bank we spoke to, which did not want to be named, introduced working from home in one of its operations as contingency planning when a deadly outbreak of swine flu in Mexico disrupted business travel and forced some air passengers into quarantine in mid-2009.

Previously, there had been a stigma attached to working at home. However, the manager of the operation decided that it made sense for people to do this, rather than to work together at an expensive remote location, especially in the event of a contagious illness outbreak.

Each team had to have one in five members working from home for a week at a time over several months to understand the benefits and address any challenges. Feelings of isolation were overcome by creative use of technology, such as instant messaging. Managers, too, were required to work from home at least one day a month or lose their remote access to office computer systems.

From office to virtual business

When Mark Thomas set up Word Association as a marketing and PR agency, he took on staff and opened an office in Leicester, England. After a few years of growing the business, he decided to take a 'sabbatical' year and travel around Europe with his young family in a motor home. He kept in touch with the UK by phone and email so he could still be involved at a distance.

When he returned, he questioned why his employees needed to be in the office at all. If he could run the business from hundreds of miles away, why couldn't his people also be remotely located? So he closed the office down and everyone started working from home. A decade later, he is running a flourishing business with 13 people working from home.

'We've never looked back,' he says. 'Staff numbers and turnover have doubled in that time and we have high levels of productivity and staff satisfaction and very low levels of absenteeism.'

As a creative business, Word Association needs people to share ideas and work together on client projects. They hold weekly progress meetings to exchange information, but otherwise rely on instant messaging and phone conversations. According to Thomas, 'it's also a way of working which keeps our overheads low, enabling us to offer our clients more for less. In the current economic times we think that more companies should be looking at our business model.'

Healthy, motivated people

Work in itself is generally good for people's health, but relentlessly long hours of work can lead to major health problems. A recent study of middle-aged British government workers, published online by the *European Heart Journal*, found a 60 percent greater risk of a heart attack or other serious cardiac disease in those who regularly worked 10–11 hour days, compared with those working a 7-hour day.[15]

Much has been written in the past decade about the increasing incidence of work-related stress and 'burnout'. Sylvia Ann Hewlett of the Center for Work–Life Policy in New York has described the proliferation of 'extreme jobs', involving 70-hour weeks, heavy travel and intense performance pressures. These jobs are particularly prevalent in financial and professional services firms but also in senior roles in many large companies. Interestingly, though, 75 percent of respondents to her research survey said they loved their jobs: the pace, the financial rewards, the recognition and the intellectual challenge.[16]

What motivates employees and keeps them engaged – or does the opposite – is a complicated matter. But we know from research that having control over one's work is a crucial factor. A 2003 study of workers in Sweden found that those with highly demanding jobs and very little latitude over how they carried out their work had an increased risk of long-term illness.[17]

In a nine-year longitudinal study in Japan, researchers found that lack of control at work was a predictor of suicides among male workers. They concluded that this finding 'implies that job redesign aimed at increased worker control could be a worthwhile strategy in preventing, or at least reducing, the risk of suicide death'.[18] As our economies become increasingly reliant on people working long beyond traditional retirement age, it will become more important than ever to address the causes of work-related physical and mental illness.

Progressive organizations have a shrewd understanding of the importance of employee motivation, or engagement, in improving customer service and thence the bottom line. They also know that winning contracts, especially in the public sector, increasingly depends on being able to demonstrate that they treat their people well and respect their needs for balanced lives.

Those companies that have bothered to measure it have found that levels of engagement are linked to the degree of autonomy people have at work. 'Flexible workers have some of the highest scores in **IBM** around the work environment,' says Gary Kildare, head of human resources at the global technology giant. 'They're generally more satisfied with their jobs and they have a greater sense of accomplishment. They tend to rate the company more highly as an employer and they're often the least likely to leave.'[19]

At **Cisco**, global focus groups, exit surveys and a regular 'Pulse' survey of employees all show that work flexibility is one of the top two issues affecting how engaged people are. 'Flexible workers have engagement scores that are three points higher on average than traditional workers,' says James Brooks, director of employee engagement and leader of flexible work initiatives.

Internal studies on employee turnover show that workers who have flexibility have a lower rate of voluntary attrition and a greater intent to stay with the company. 'Employees respond very well to the opportunity to customise their work and manage it in a way that enables them to integrate their work and lives. Providing this type of self-direction and flexibility builds employee engagement and passion for their work.'[20]

This kind of drive is something that **Google** has turned into a distinct source of innovation among its large workforce of engineers. Competition for jobs at the world's biggest internet company is fierce and it seeks to recruit already highly motivated self-achievers who are capable of working collaboratively. People are judged on results, not hours, says Matt Brittin, head of operations in the UK and Ireland. 'Our engineers can work whatever hours they like, assuming they coordinate with colleagues and deliver what they've agreed. They can be nocturnal.'

Engineers have a large degree of latitude and control over their work, with the option to spend 20 percent of their time on a project of their own devising. Gmail, the internet mailing service, and Google News were two services that resulted from this practice. It can be frustrating for managers when engineers go off to work on their own ideas, admits Brittin. 'But it's not having 20 percent time of your time to muck about. It's mainly for engineers to be able to be creative and pursue their passions, and to do that within Google rather than having to leave.'[21]

Saving the planet

As we described in Chapter 1, many people are motivated to work by factors other than the financial reward. There are employees of all ages, not just in Gen Y, who want to feel part of an organization that cares about its environmental impact and about addressing wider social challenges.

Future work practices make organizations more attractive institutions to work for, or to be connected with. They also produce big environmental benefits.

BT says its agile working strategy has reduced employees' commuting time by 1800 years, saving 12m liters of fuel.[22]

Cisco also measures the environmental gains. Employees who use its Virtual Office software avoid 36.4 commuting miles on average for each work-at-home day, totaling 47m miles a year, it says. This means a reduction in auto emissions of 22,710 tons of CO_2 annually, saving nearly $126,000 per year in reforestation project costs necessary to offset the automobile carbon footprint.[23]

Studies by the US Telework Research Network show the environmental benefits that would result if the 40 percent of Americans who could work away from the office actually did so for half of the time. 'Each person could save an average of $362 on gas per year [at $2.40 a gallon],' says the Network's Kate Lister. 'At the national level, that adds up to over $15bn in savings a year. It would reduce US greenhouse gas emissions by about 53m metric tons – that's the equivalent of taking more than 9.6m cars off the road for one year.'[24]

Increased use of broadband and home-working in the US could reduce greenhouse gas emissions by 28m tons due to less office construction, and 312m tons through energy saved by businesses, according to the American Consumer Institute.[25]

In the UK, home-working twice a week by UK workers with compatible jobs and a desire to do so would reduce greenhouse gases by the equivalent of taking 2.5m cars off the road and save over £750m a year in imported oil, says a separate study by the Telework Research Network.[26]

Adding it all up

Unfortunately, few organizations currently measure the business benefits of future work at all, let alone in any detail. BDO USA, which we featured at the start of this chapter, is unusual in having collected a large amount of data on a wide range of business and people benefits, including cost savings, increased speed to market, productivity gains and improved employee morale.

We examine these under the two headings: tangible and intangible benefits. As a case study, it neatly encapsulates many of the advantages that we have covered in this chapter.

Tangible business gains:

- Real estate savings: The firm's new offices in big urban centers are making creative use of office space, telecommuting and coordination of team schedules to help manage the high cost of real estate. As well as the Manhattan example, the firm's chief financial officer, Howard Allenberg, calculates that annual savings from individuals who work exclusively from their homes or clients' offices, compared with having dedicated BDO office space, amounts to $500,000–$700,000 a year in reduced facility and equipment rentals, maintenance and related occupancy costs.

- Rapid moves into new markets: The firm says it entered and grew faster in new markets, such as Austin, Texas, by making flexible use of telecommuting rather than taking on physical office space at the start. Professionals who lived in Austin but worked at the Houston office began to work from their own or each other's homes or clients' offices in Austin to help develop the business quickly, says Marcee Harris Schwartz of BDO. This saved about $1.6m in office overheads in the first three years until the business was solid enough to justify opening physical premises.[27]

■ Extended service cover: The new working models are not confined to accountancy professionals at BDO. Some administrative staff work part of the time from home or do shifts so they come in and leave at different times, says Harris Schwartz. 'Three admin assistants in the Dallas office do a rotating schedule, each working a compressed week every third week, which involves four 10-hour days, while the other two do normal eight-hour days.' This not only benefited them but also provided extended cover for the partners, and it saved money because the firm did not have to pay the staff overtime to stay extra hours. The IT department used flexible schedules and telecommuting to extend its Help Desk user support from the traditional 7.30 a.m.–7.30 p.m. Eastern Time to any time of the day, regardless of where users are located.

Intangible business gains:

It is harder to isolate the impact of the Flex Strategy on things like hiring and employee turnover, but BDO runs a regular survey of employees which is a useful guide to how people feel about the firm, their own productivity and how well they are able to balance their work with the rest of their lives.

The 2009 employee survey found that the strategy positively impacted:

■ Their work–life balance (72 percent said it did)
■ Their desire to stay with the firm (71 percent)
■ Their productivity (70 percent)
■ The firm's ability to recruit talent (83 percent)
■ The firm's ability to keep talent (82 percent)
■ The firm's ability to compete in the global market (74 percent)
■ The firm's ability to serve clients (65 percent)

BDO has found ways to do better business in a highly competitive sector. As Harris Schwartz says: 'It's a reality for anyone working in the professional services industry that clients want access when they want access. But I don't think that means one individual has to be available to them at all times. We have examples of teams being more thoughtful about creating multiple relationships with clients so that they can extend their availability, for example by offering the clients the possibility of reaching one of three people.'

Crucially, the firm's CEO, Jack Weisbaum, leads by example, working from his home office in Florida when he is not traveling. 'As the CEO of a national accounting firm, I travel extensively and have a great deal of demand for my time,' he told us. 'Having the ability to work from home and manage my time has

enabled me to stay involved professionally, stay active within my community and
participate in both social and charity events. It has really enhanced my ability to
work, while also enjoying a rewarding personal life with my wife and family.
In the past, someone in my situation would have retired by now or faced the risk
of losing many of the things they hold near and dear.'

Chapter 5 looks at how other senior people in highly demanding jobs in
different industries around the world are showing that future work makes
business and personal sense for them too.

Leaders of the future

If you're going to be a successful leader, you should be able to take on more things without adding to your hours because you will know how to engage, empower and trust other people to do the work. In turn, employees who are given greater autonomy will be more productive, healthier and more committed to their jobs.

Murray Martin, chairman and CEO, Pitney Bowes[1]

At his home in California's Santa Cruz mountains, nearly two hours' drive up winding roads from San Francisco, Slade Fester is living proof that people can hold down a senior job regardless of where, when and how they do their work.

Thanks to technology, an enlightened employer and an adaptable personal style, Fester, a partner with an international accountancy firm, is able to satisfy the competing demands of his clients, his team of 20 auditors and managers and his young family. He even finds time to pursue his passion of ocean surfing when the swell hits the Pacific coast.

'In some respects, I'm working round-the-clock because a lot of my clients are international companies – I do a lot of calls and emails in the evening, which is beneficial because I'll get an answer from someone in Europe or China while I'm sleeping,' he says. 'Within that 24-hour day, however, I'm also getting really valuable quality time with my family and surfing. Sometimes I'm out on the ocean four to five times a week.'[2]

No two days are the same for the 49-year-old Fester. He works a day or two from home each week. On the other days, he drives to visit clients or to see colleagues at the San Francisco and San José offices of his firm, BDO USA.

Living and working so remotely (even the nearest store is 20 minutes' drive from the house), he makes it a priority to strengthen relationships with people during his city visits. 'I'll do whatever it takes to show up face-to-face for the key meetings,' he says. 'In the office, I roam the floor and drop in to see people in their cubes.' Unlike more traditional office-based colleagues who spend most of their time at their computers, he does his concentrated work at home, often after his children have gone to bed.

Can there be life at the top?

There's a powerfully prevalent view in the business world that holding down a senior executive role is incompatible with 'having a life'. This belief is perpetuated by many of those currently in power. Here's what John Rowe, chairman and CEO of Exelon, a large US energy company, told a conference of diversity professionals in 2009: 'If you're going to have a very senior job at a very high-performance company, it requires a near totality of commitment. There's some level in most government or corporate structures where balance becomes near impossible.'[3]

Conventional flexible working arrangements, typically based on the number of hours or days worked per week or year, remain a 'no-go' area for executives in many organizations. Three-quarters of European Union companies have no part-timers in highly qualified or managerial positions, according to one survey.[4] Another study found that managers in Britain and other countries were often excluded from 'part-time' jobs. Nearly one in five UK employers in the retail sector – which could not function without flexibility from its employees – made 'full-time' work a condition of managerial posts. Not surprisingly, managers were found to be less likely than other employees to ask to reduce their hours and, if they did, were more likely to be turned down.[5]

'Flexibility in senior jobs is the most difficult area,' acknowledges Caroline Waters, who is director of people and policy at BT, a UK communications company that has done more than most to enable people to work remotely and enjoy a degree of autonomy over their working patterns. 'There are a lot of extreme jobs in industry. We need more senior people sharing jobs and working part time to create the role models that will make this a more common solution right across industry. The question companies need to ask is: "Do we want this extremely able person for some of the time, or not at all?" because they may very well go elsewhere if we cannot give them that flexibility.'

We would argue that companies also need to ask why they still judge senior people on presence and hours worked, rather than performance. There's no doubt that people running large organizations need to be driven, focused and hardworking. It is illogical, however, given the latitude that technology now allows in the way we work, to equate these requirements with having to sacrifice any semblance of a personal life.

There's a danger that these myths about the need for body-and-soul commitment to the corporation will undermine the future success of business. This is because they risk alienating people with the leadership skills for a world in which operations and teams are dispersed across regions and time zones: balanced leaders who encourage collaboration, understand people, know how to motivate them and are open to innovative work practices.

Gender and generational shifts

In Chapter 4, we listed 'stronger management skills' among the intangible business gains associated with future work. Technical proficiency is not enough in the new world of work. More than ever, managers need strong people skills. Those who have these attributes, or who acquire them, should do well. Those who lack them will find their credibility and their position eroded. The organizations that make a successful transition to future work will be those that value such skills and encourage their growth.

INSEAD, the international business school, looked at ten 'critical components' of leadership and found that female executives received higher ratings than male executives in most of them. These ten components overlap with many of the attributes we believe managers need to succeed in the future world of work. They are: envisioning; empowering; energizing; designing and aligning; rewarding and feedback; team building; outside orientation; global mindset; tenacity; and emotional intelligence. Women were rated more highly than men by their bosses, peers and subordinates on all of these except envisioning, empowering and global mindset. On the latter two, neither men nor women stood out as being better.[6]

These findings support the already substantial case for greater gender balance in top teams, since people who possess these leadership attributes will be particularly well-placed to manage and lead in the new world of work.

A separate study found a link between female leadership and trust. During the economic crisis, chief executives who protected jobs through creative approaches, such as flexible working and budget cuts, saw their trust scores rise, according to a survey of 5000 managers and employees by the UK's Institute of Leadership & Management, in collaboration with *Management Today* magazine. CEOs who instituted the most severe cutbacks, such as job losses and site closures, suffered a sharp drop in trust.

Women leaders scored more highly than their male counterparts on average. 'Our research indicates this is because female CEOs display a more pronounced interest in and concern for employees at all levels,' said David Pardey, the institute's head of research and policy. 'There is a lesson here for male CEOs to ponder – by demonstrating more interest in and awareness of the roles of the people they lead, they could enhance their levels of leadership trust.'[7]

There are interesting echoes here of the teachings of Mary Parker Follett, one of the early female management gurus, who wrote nearly 100 years ago about the importance of employee involvement and the exercise of 'power with' people instead of 'power over' them.

Beyond crisis management, leaders need to understand how work is changing, both in terms of technology and the physical environment and in terms of workforce attitudes. A report on twenty-first century leadership 'essentials' by The Conference Board, the global business membership and research organization, points to the changing nature of work and expectations of the workforce. It says that leaders need to:

- recognize that individuals are more powerful than ever, with networks that transcend corporate boundaries
- understand employees' different motivations
- make flexibility a corporate value
- be comfortable with non-traditional career paths[8]

The importance of such adaptability is recognized by Karen Newton, a managing director at Credit Suisse, the Swiss banking group, in London, who has promoted remote working in her team. 'Some managers say that it's more difficult to manage people that they can't see,' she says. 'I say to them: "Look around at our senior staff. Most of them have responsibility for people across different geographies. They can't see where their team is at any one time." '

Managers now regard the ability to manage people on a remote basis as 'an extra string to their bow', she says. 'People now talk about having remote workers on their team with a sense of pride and achievement. They say: "I'm preparing myself for a global role or for managing a geographically dispersed team."'

In our research for this book, we have found strong signs of a reaction against the pervasive notion that presence equals commitment. Younger leaders, in particular, appear to be less willing to play by the old rules. There is pent-up demand for greater autonomy, both for themselves and for their teams. Our survey of managers found that 58 percent want more freedom to let their teams work more flexibly, and over half also want more control over where, when and how they do their own jobs.

Younger managers appear less willing to sacrifice personal interests and responsibilities in the pursuit of leadership. They do not understand why this should be necessary. Indeed, some see it as their responsibility as leaders to demonstrate that a balanced life is possible and healthy.

This chapter shows how you, as a leader today or in the future, can benefit personally, and help your organization benefit, from future work. It tells the stories of six pioneering leaders from different sectors and countries, how they developed their individual working arrangements, and what lessons they have learned about managing teams and businesses successfully in the 24/7 world.

Some have had to battle against entrenched attitudes in their organization or sector, while others like Fester deliberately chose to work in a corporate environment that encourages new work models and implicitly understands the benefits for people and business. They have these common features:

- They are strongly committed to their clients
- They value their personal lives
- They trust the people who work for them
- They want to change organizational life for the better

Finding the right 'fit': Slade Fester

Fester is a leading figure in the 'People Force' initiative, started in the San Francisco Bay Area offices about five years ago. 'Its aim is to empower people – staff and managers – to make BDO a better place to work,' he says. 'We realized that constant communication was essential in order to give equal attention to developing the business, managing resources and keeping people engaged. We have fortnightly teleconferences with staff from every level to solicit their thoughts about the mood of the office as well as topics relating to the business and resources. Employees voice their concerns and help to develop solutions to the issues raised.'

Like him, some employees live far from the office or have family responsibilities. He advises people on finding 'the right fit'. He also works with fellow partners who feel uncomfortable not having a manager or staff member physically present in the office all the time.

'In situations like these, it really just takes a tweak of the approach and an adjustment of attitude to make it work,' he says. 'It may be better coordination or communication when in the office. One of our star performers was grappling with his "long distance relationship" with work. To make his periodic visits to the office more meaningful and productive, he needed to cluster his meetings, make sure he was there for the key ones, and be more visible instead of spending all the time inside his own office. These were things that I found were helpful in my similar situation.'

Organizations that grant people autonomy are more likely to keep the talent they need. Fester is a case in point. He took a circuitous career route to seniority – something we expect to become far more common as organizational structures change and working lives last longer.

After college and five years working for the accountancy firm then known as Coopers & Lybrand, he took a year's sabbatical to travel the world with his surfboard. When he returned home, friends who had moved to BDO lured him there with talk of its flexible culture. During his first years with the firm, he worked for six months of the year and spent the other six months surfing. Even after becoming a full-time employee 15 years ago, he took time out to build the house in the mountains, where he lives with his wife Reyna, a creative writer, and two children.

He sees his lifestyle as the only way to cope with the 'always on' world of work of the early twenty-first century. 'With technology, and with the world getting smaller and smaller, everyone's expected to get more and more done,' he says. '*How* you get it done is the question. I wouldn't still be doing a full-time corporate job if I wasn't able to release the pressure valves by going surfing or having these quality moments with my family. I'd make my own flexibility by doing my own thing as an entrepreneur.'

Change in an inflexible profession: Monica Burch

The City of London is hardly known as a hub of innovation when it comes to working patterns. Each day, hundreds of thousands of employees squeeze grimly into overcrowded underground trains and fight their way up escalators to their office blocks in the morning rush hour. Global competition and high rewards go hand in hand with old-fashioned, inflexible work practices and the pressure to be seen at your desk for long hours.

So Monica Burch's achievement in becoming the first woman to chair Addleshaw Goddard, a leading commercial law firm with 1300 employees, is all the more remarkable. In 2010, Burch stood for election as head of the business and was chosen by her fellow equity partners. She made it clear in the election process that she would continue to work 90 percent, rather than 100 percent, of the year. This was what she had done since the arrival of her third child seven years earlier, and she was determined to keep space for her family as she took over the running of the firm.

Burch believes that setting a visible example is crucial to secure the talent on which the business depends for the future. When she joined the firm in 1988, women and men were already entering the legal profession in equal numbers.

'Now, 65 per cent of entry-level graduates are women. So there's a huge demographic issue,' she says. 'Thirty-three is the age when professional women tend to have children and it's traditionally the age when you look at becoming a partner. Women are either going before they start families, or they are saying: "I can't make this work" and are leaving later on.' Many of these women go to work in-house for corporate clients where the hours are a bit more predictable.

'Purely from a business perspective, you want to be able to pick the best people,' she says. 'It's not very good business practice if you cut off one large part of that talent.'[9]

Clients, especially those in the public sector, are demanding evidence of 'diversity' from law firms that work for them. Women represent 22 percent of Addleshaw Goddard's 180 partners. 'For our industry, that's on the good side of our peer group, and yet it's appalling when you think that lawyers all start the same way, with the same levels of qualifications, and the same training. It makes it more shocking when you look at the numbers, because partnerships are so broad. There are 12,000 partners in the UK's top 20 firms. It's not like trying to get onto a corporate board of directors where there are a far smaller number of seats.'

Her firm is unusual in treating flexible working as a smart business move, rather than a concession to employees. It has made a significant investment in IT, with BlackBerrys, laptops and electronic key fobs available to all staff who want them, so that people can log in securely while working away from the office. As well as formal flexible working arrangements, used by 16 percent of staff, most people have some informal autonomy over where they work. Working from home is 'pretty accepted and usual', she says.

The number of senior (equity) partners working flexibly is still fairly small – five men and four women out of 100 – but Burch believes this is a good start. The firm is attracting more female talent: half of the partners recruited from outside in the past three years have been women. Elizabeth Robertson, a partner who joined in 2007 and specializes in corporate crime and regulation, says: 'I was surprised to find flexibility so deeply embedded within a law firm and in such a commercially minded way.'[10]

Burch confesses that it is unusual for highly rewarded commercial lawyers 'to ever completely switch off'. Her own schedule is extremely demanding, even on a 90 percent contract. She typically works 11–12 hour days and usually has events with clients in the evenings. She uses the days she accumulates under her contract to take longer chunks of leave during school holidays or to have occasional days off during the term to attend sports days and children's concerts.

What will it take for the legal profession to move to a culture that judges people on results, not hours? As an advocate of change, she sees two major obstacles. One is the unpredictability of some of the work. Clients involved in corporate transactions such as mergers and acquisitions need their lawyers to work until the deal is done. This can mean several days non-stop without sleep.

The chief obstacle is the system of billing clients by the hour. 'The measure of productivity is the number of hours worked,' she says. 'The more you do, the better you are. In the traditional law firm model, the partner sits surrounded by their team, who feel they have to be in place, with their jackets on the chairs, until the partner leaves in the evening. Most law firms are grappling with this. There's a big debate about what's the best model for billing clients. If hourly billing is kicked into touch and you price by output, it will be easier to change the culture.'

Over the past three years, with leadership from the top, the firm has worked to shift attitudes and challenge assumptions. 'We have accepted flexible working as part of the culture and focused on performance, not hours worked,' says Burch. 'When we look at promotions to partner, the working pattern of the candidate simply doesn't come into it. That's a real change for us.'

Having to manage people working away from the office has been good for the business. 'If you don't have all your ducks in a row all the time, it makes people better managers. You have to think more broadly. It makes you more agile and better able to respond to clients because you are better able to cope with not having everyone lined up and waiting for the work.'

She believes attitudes are changing, albeit slowly. 'Some law firms want 2500 charged and billed hours a year from their lawyers as a matter of course. I think people in the future will look back and say: "How did we put up with that?" in the same way that we look back now at the practice of sending children up chimneys and say: "How could people have put up with that?" '

Shared leadership: Carolyn Davidson and Tom Carter

The past 40 years have seen a dramatic rise in dual-earning couples. Women have become the majority of university graduates in many countries, and higher education has boosted their earning power. More than 20 percent of US wives today earn more than their husbands, up from just 4 percent in 1970.[11]

These trends, while in many ways liberating, have created complications for couples and their employers with regard to international assignments. The main cause of failed assignments is partner dissatisfaction, and nearly half of people who turn down postings cite their partner's career as the reason, according to a survey of global relocation trends.[12]

In the British Foreign Office, as in diplomatic services around the world, promotion depends on readiness to take up foreign postings. So when one high-flying diplomatic couple, Carolyn Davidson and Tom Carter, were unable to find a ready-made way to combine their careers with bringing up their children, they invented one.

Neither wanted to stop working completely, so they came up with the idea of a novel job-share in which they would take it in turns to switch from the diplomatic to the home role every four months. After meeting some initial resistance, they were granted the post of Deputy Head of Mission in Slovakia in 2003. They achieved the balance they were seeking and their young sons took the arrangement in their stride. At work, the experiment proved so successful that in 2008 they were appointed joint British High Commissioner to Zambia – the world's first job-sharing heads of mission.

In a phone interview with them in Lusaka, their working relationship is immediately evident as they answer questions alternately and give each other space to comment.[13]

'We take it in turns to lead, for four month stints,' explains Davidson. 'We work on the strategic stuff together, but the one "in the seat" at the time does the day-to-day implementation. We take special care in the run-up to handovers to brief the incomer on all live issues. We make a point of going round the High Commission and making ourselves known again, making it clear that there's been a change of sex! What people have commented on in our 360-degree feedback to managers is that it's a very seamless transition every four months.'

They have also been told their joint problem-solving ability is notably better than one person's working alone. Is this a future leadership model for couples working for the same organization? 'I think it is,' says Carter. 'You end up with a better set of decisions if there are two of you doing it. You get a much more comprehensive approach to an issue.'

There are other benefits for the organization. The Foreign Office has retained talent. 'If we hadn't done the job share and Tom had got another posting, I'd have been out of the office for seven years,' says Davidson. 'Experience dictates that people who are out for that long don't tend to come back.'

The arrangement has generated positive publicity for Britain's diplomatic service, depicting it as an innovative employer in the media and in the eyes of counterparts from countries such as Sweden, Russia and China.

The main risk with any such arrangement would be if the couple's personal relationship broke down, and with it the job-share. However, marital splits can interfere with work and jeopardize overseas assignments, regardless of the working model.

The Foreign Office has two heads for the price of one, an advantage particularly when budgets are being severely squeezed. The financial side has been the main drawback for Carter and Davidson, who traded their double incomes for a single one split between two. Now that their children are older, they are contemplating another innovation whereby they might take on two full-time jobs, one in the diplomatic service, and the other on secondment to the private sector, on a four-monthly rotation.

Like most government departments, the Foreign Office wants people to gain experience in the private sector that they can bring back into the organization. 'If we could combine doing that with what we've learned from doing the job-share, it would be a powerful model of future leadership,' says Carter.

Challenges of promotion: Chris Ainslie

Promotion can pose a particular challenge for managers who pioneer future work. With the extra responsibilities and money often comes pressure to be highly 'visible', especially if you are in the running for one of the top jobs. Holding out for your principles becomes tougher the more senior you get, as Chris Ainslie found.

For four and a half years, Ainslie ran a £500m turnover business unit within BT, the big UK-based telecoms group, while working four days a week. As an ambitious vice-president, he put in ten-hour days, but on Thursday nights he switched off his phone and laptop to spend Friday and the weekend focusing on the rest of his life.

He had insisted on this arrangement as a condition of accepting the job when he was headhunted to the company. It took guts, since no one at his level of seniority had done anything like this. But he was determined to stand up to entrenched attitudes. He had lost his twin brother to a brain tumor in his 30s and realized that life was too short, and too precious, to miss out on being a father to his young family. 'Up till then, I was working a 70-hour week and was the proverbial "virtual" parent who just provided the cash,' he says.[14]

Revenues and profit margins in his business unit rose during his tenure, as did employee satisfaction scores. His working arrangement also produced unexpected benefits. His team of seven managers took it in turns to stand in for him on Fridays, getting a chance to show off their leadership skills and aiding the company's succession planning.

He became a role model inside and outside the firm, attracting questions from other executives about how to do it and boosting BT's reputation for flexibility. 'There's a deep interest because talent is becoming a very powerful part of any business,' he said in a *Financial Times* interview.[15] 'Companies must recognize that to keep talent they need to be more creative in their approach. Money is not the only driver.'

Then in 2009 he won promotion within BT Global Services to run a division that provides IT services to local governments across the UK. From managing 250 people, he took over a far more complex business with 3300 people and an annual turnover of £700m. 'When you lead in a different way, you get asked to do bigger things,' he says.[16] 'By empowering staff and trusting their competence and judgment – that is, truly delegating – the whole business ecosystem is enhanced, more capable and more motivated. It allows people to find more fulfillment and have a bit more fun and they tend to deliver more.'

Reluctantly, the 43-year-old reverted to a full-on working week. 'The market has changed massively with local government budget cuts,' he explains. 'The business I've taken over is in challenging shape and needs more focus than I could give in a four-day week, with a team that is relatively new. I had the big aspiration to get the job back to a four-day week with the support of the then president, who has left to be a CEO elsewhere. The new regime has not been as flexible as I was hoping. But I still have that aspiration.'

Yet he continues to make time for family life, using technology to the full and being fiercely disciplined. Interestingly, he has moved from the rigidity of a formal flexible working arrangement – in his case, a 'compressed working week' – to more of an 'anytime, anywhere' model. His working life now more closely resembles that of Slade Fester at the start of this chapter.

In his previous job, he stayed away from home in the city every Monday to Wednesday night. Now he spends more time traveling back and forth and working on the train. He makes phone calls, conference calls and uses his laptop with a 3G card for mobile internet access. 'With the company's flexible working technology it's exactly like being in the office, with my email, desktop, and Web favorites. I have to be careful, however, not to do any publicly sensitive or confidential work on the train.'

Every Friday, he works at home, which enables him to drop his children off at school and pick them up. 'I go to parents' evenings and rugby matches. On Monday this week, I was working from home. I was up at 7am, did half an hour's work, had breakfast with the boys, then worked from 8am through to when my wife got home about 6pm. I had dinner with the boys, helped one with his chemistry homework and went to see the other playing trumpet in a band. After that I worked a bit more until 9.30pm.'

To manage a high-pressure job and maintain a family life, Ainslie says he:

- Prioritizes tasks ruthlessly
- Delegates as much as possible
- Focuses on customer needs each day before opening his inbox
- Never handles an email more than once
- Makes decisions quickly
- Has his phone and laptop switched off from Friday evening to Monday morning

A wider pool of leaders: Isla Ramos Chaves

Isla Ramos Chaves has no doubt that the business world will change significantly as future work becomes more commonplace. 'It will take us to more diverse organizations in the widest sense,' says the director of strategy and business operations in Western Europe for Lenovo, the Chinese-owned PC manufacturer. 'It's important for international businesses to have people in their leadership team who know about other markets and have a different way of thinking, rather than the old model of leadership where it was always the same people holding the same positions. It opens the door to so many possibilities.'[17]

Her own experience, as a woman and a Spaniard on the European board of the company, illustrates the point perfectly. An ex-IBMer, she moved to Lenovo when it was spun off from the US parent group in 2005. Having done various international assignments, she wanted to stay in Madrid to be near her ailing mother. The ability to do the job remotely, rather than to move to Lenovo's West European headquarters in Paris, was the deciding factor in accepting the promotion.

'I wouldn't have taken this job if I'd had to move to Paris,' she says. 'The conditions of the job offer were important because it's really difficult for a Spanish person who doesn't want to move abroad permanently to get a senior position in a multinational company. These jobs are usually in the larger countries or big hubs.'

Leaders in international businesses today must have the skills to manage people scattered across different countries and time zones. 'It's not an optional model any more,' she says. 'If you're going to make the most of your global resources you don't have any alternative. Big fat headquarters are no longer affordable for many companies, and they're not very agile. Learning how to manage people remotely needs to be embedded in every management-training program: it takes a lot more work to lead remotely than on site.'

Ramos Chaves, 40, spends most of her time working from a Lenovo office in Madrid, but none of her 80-strong team is based there. They work in different European countries, some from home, and some from satellite offices, depending on the culture. Unlike the UK, for example, working from home is uncommon in Spain.

Making the move from office-based to remote working can be challenging. She now encourages her team to spend time in their local office with colleagues. 'Some people go crazy if they're working on their own. There's a level of uncertainty that they can't handle. They may need constant reassurance, and you need to be very aware of that. When you're agreeing objectives, you need to see if it suits them.'

However, she has found the ability to work autonomously has had an equally positive impact on both men and women. People have become much more productive because they can choose the most effective time to do particular tasks, rather than having to work in a fixed location for a fixed schedule.

'It has empowered and developed the members of the team significantly. Many of them have developed incredible levels of autonomy and this has changed their approach to work completely, to being much more proactive and solution-oriented.'

She says future work practices will only be successful if:

- They are treated as a competitive advantage and embedded in the business strategy. 'It will be unsustainable if it isn't spread across the organization and seen as part of the way you do business.'

- The organization is set up to enable remote working. 'Being equipped with the right tools is essential.'
- Communication with team members is made an absolute priority. 'It requires really high doses of discipline.'

She communicates with her team by phone, email, teleconferencing and videoconferencing, online chats and instant messages. She makes a point of sticking to scheduled call times. 'It's about them knowing where they stand in their communication with you. With a new person, I tell them that I don't always answer the phone because I'm very busy, but they should leave a message and I'll get back. Then they are not left with the anguish of not knowing where they stand. You have to create a virtual space with people: so you say, for example: "On Monday between 9am and 10am I'm all yours. Whatever happens, this is the time we spend together." '

In summary

The pioneers featured in this chapter offer many lessons for leadership in the twenty-first century world of work. They demonstrate strong principles, a curiosity about how to get the best out of people, and an ability to learn and adapt.

To be an innovative role model and to lead a flexible team requires:

- Well-honed communication skills
- Efficient use of time
- Ability to delegate and trust people
- Prioritizing tasks and meetings that matter
- Willingness to challenge the status quo
- Understanding that no one size fits all
- Discipline about 'switching off'
- Accepting the need to adapt your thinking

We give detailed guidance on the skills that managers and leaders need to develop in Chapters 8 and 9. In Chapter 6, we investigate the changing role of location in work, and the implications this has for management.

Changing workplaces

The office should be a meeting place, not a working place. We can work anywhere, so it is social cohesion that becomes the important factor in physical premises.

Theo Rinsema, general manager, Microsoft Netherlands

Does the office have a future?

The entrance to the **Microsoft** building in Amsterdam, a huge reflective-glass box next to Schiphol Airport, has the feel of an ultra-modern hotel lobby. People sit and stand around, chatting or waiting for appointments, bags and suitcases on the floor and laptops open on tables. Low sofas and coffee beckon from the hospitality corner.

There is no traditional reception desk with fixed phones. Black-suited receptionists emerge from behind a long white counter, greeting visitors, offering refreshments and using handheld messaging devices to alert hosts to their guests' arrival. Only the security barriers to the lifts and stairs signal that this is corporate territory.

The Netherlands office, designed for a world in which work is independent of time and location, is an experiment for Microsoft. Since it opened in 2008, it has attracted 500–1000 visitors a week, eager to glimpse the physical embodiment of 'anytime anywhere' work. Similar new Microsoft sites have followed in Belgium, France and Norway, and there has been interest from Argentina, Australia, India, Japan and Switzerland. The most common questions visitors ask are what it means for the individual, for productivity and for leadership.

Theo Rinsema, the Netherlands general manager, explains the concept behind the new design. With 'anytime anywhere' work, the role of the physical office changes, he says. Instead of being the location where employees gather at fixed times to do concentrated work, it becomes primarily a place for developing and maintaining connections between people.[1]

On the first floor, color takes over from the black-and-white décor of the lobby. This is the 'community' floor, full of meeting spaces and people. The atmosphere is purposeful but informal. The busy restaurant has three-sided booths, with low-hanging lights over the tables. One long wall is covered with sound-absorbing, green fabric pieces held in place by what look like buttons.

At the far end of the floor is a series of meeting rooms with sofas, chairs and poufs but few tables, encouraging people to sink into whatever sitting, or even lying, position, they find most comfortable. There are tiny red chambers for private phone calls, and a wall of lockers with individuals' names chalked, kindergarten-style, on the doors.

Every employee has a badge with a chip inside which gives them access to the building and to all corporate information stored digitally, apart from personnel files. 'Connectedness' is emphasized by the open view from the first floor down into the lobby and up to the quieter second floor, which is dedicated to client meeting rooms. Here there are small workstations with sliding glass doors for concentrated, individual work, and open-plan desks that can be raised or lowered for preference.

Sevil Peach, the architect who led the design of the Microsoft building, says the future is about 'empowering people to make decisions about how they want to work throughout a day'.[2]

With the growth of mobile working around the world, the purpose of the bricks-and-mortar office is under scrutiny. There is pressure on organizations to reduce their carbon footprint, and potentially large scope to do so while making cost savings on office space if employees are spending more time working away from their desks.

Employees' expectations are adding to that pressure. According to an international survey commissioned by Cisco Systems, the networking technology company, 60 percent of people believe they do not need to be in an office to be productive, a view that is strongest among employees in India, China and Brazil. Based on these findings, Cisco asks: 'Is the office really necessary?'[3]

The answer is yes, but not in its conventional form. We do not expect, unlike some of the wilder predictions made back in the 1980s, that everyone will work from home and that offices will disappear any time soon. Even in the most technologically advanced companies like Microsoft, people are still social animals. Humans need to meet face-to-face, at least in early encounters, to develop fruitful relationships. Moreover, some people find solitary work difficult and stressful, while others thrive on it. What's important for most people is to have a healthy mix.

'People like the choice of working at home but they often go spare if they are there for more than a couple of days a week,' says Alexi Marmot, professor of environment and facility management at University College

London. 'There aren't many jobs that even the most thoughtful people can work at for weeks on end without the company of others. You somehow get empowered by the presence of other people. Evolutionary biologists and psychologists say that mankind is generally equipped to live in social groups.'[4]

Online collaboration can be highly successful, but there are times when we have to be together in person to make things work. Advanced video-conferencing technology can simulate everyone being in the same room, even when they are dispersed around the globe, and it is becoming a good substitute for expensive and time-consuming business travel. But it cannot entirely replace the energy that people derive from each other's physical presence, or the more personal, thoughtful discussions that bond colleagues and collaborators and make people feel valued.

Offices will continue to be an important feature of the twenty-first century landscape. But the role of location in work is changing significantly, and with it the role of management.

In this chapter we examine some emerging workplace models, their benefits and limitations and the changes they require in management attitudes and behavior. We give examples from around the world including Macquarie in Australia, the US federal government in Washington DC, Unilever in Germany and Vodafone in the UK, starting with an in-depth look at how Microsoft's Dutch operation adapted its culture and management practices to the new world of work.

From workplace to meeting place

Employees of Microsoft in the Netherlands already had a lot of flexibility and were well-used to working from home at least part of the week, even before the move to the new building. But something was not right.

'They rated their work–life balance at 5.3 on a scale of 1 to 10 because they found it so difficult to stop working,' says Rinsema. 'So the question for us was: Have we adapted enough to this world of technology and globalization? Since we moved to the new building, the work–life balance score has gone up from 5.3 to 8.4, and is one of the highest in Microsoft worldwide.'

Productivity, measured by a model developed by Erasmus University in Rotterdam, has increased slightly following the move. The employee attrition rate is low at 8–9 percent a year, which is a mixed blessing: it demonstrates people's attachment to the new environment but it also holds back recruitment of new talent. The Dutch business wants to increase its female population, for example, from 17 percent to 25 percent by mid-2012.

The space per employee has fallen from 16 square meters to 11.5 square meters. Yet the occupancy rate has increased from just 25 percent in the previous offices to 40–45 percent, a big jump, though still below average office occupancy rates. 'We're a marketing and sales office so people should be outside,' explains Gonnie Been, manager of corporate communications and social innovation. 'But we also get our customers to visit us here.'[5]

The 600 full-time employees, as well as the 300 contractors and interim staff, work from home one day a week on average, and the rest of the time at customers' sites or the Schiphol building. Even people who have to be present in the building to do their jobs, such as the receptionists and caterers, have a degree of autonomy, as they are able to arrange their own schedules.

Central to the success of the transfer has been the leadership team's focus on changing culture and attitudes. 'When we moved to this building, we moved from control to trust,' says Rinsema. 'We manage by output rather than presence. I don't know an organization that has put so much emphasis on changing leadership styles as we have. We separated status from hierarchy. There was some resistance during the journey.'

He agrees that future work is about empowering people, making them more productive and helping them with their work–life balance, or integration. 'It was perfectly clear to me that we had to further develop our leadership style in order to unleash employee empowerment. To be capable of leading based on trust, we as leaders realized that we had to look at our personal development, especially our personal drivers and control mechanisms.'

Rinsema has used a coach and facilitator to develop his team, including himself. At the start of the sessions, he asked what the program would be. The coach told him there was no program. This turned out to be the beginning of learning to let go.

'I gained a better insight into my personal control mechanisms and how much I depend on these,' he says. 'Fortunately I also gained insight into how I could loosen up a bit. I have the perception that I am much closer to the employees, with many more interactions through a variety of media. The balance between leading on the one hand and being a networked colleague on the other hand is, in this context, crucial. Regarding the anywhere anytime workforce, you have to support and coach people that you do not expect them to be "always on". You have to set the example as a leader.'

One highly symbolic change is that there are no individual offices. This is culturally very different from Microsoft's vast US headquarters in Redmond, Washington, where enclosed individual offices generally still matter and where the software giant has made huge investments in expanding its real estate portfolio on the campus and surrounding area in recent years.[6]

'Nobody has a dedicated office, not even me,' says Rinsema. 'You find the ideal workspace depending on what you are doing.'

It is no accident that this pioneering building is in the Netherlands. It is easier to make the shift to future working styles in some cultural contexts than others. In general, northern Europe is more open to this than southern Europe, says Been. But there is resistance in America too. 'In the US, it still matters how long you have been in service, so cultural patterns are preventing it from changing,' she says. 'Europeans were more traditional and we're moving faster now. We must not become complacent. I'm working on how we get that constant change so that we stay ahead.'

One of the hardest things is breaking the link between status and position in the hierarchy. In the Netherlands, they are trying to do this by redefining status as the individual's contribution and leadership skills. People are encouraged both to move across functions and to develop individual expertise.

'Status comes through leadership, if people want to work with you,' says Been. 'The whole approach to the new world of work is that you need to be a personal leader – you need to lead your own life rather than being controlled by the boss as in the past – and if you're able to do that you are able to lead others. My next step could be towards more of a specialist role.'

One breakthrough followed an agreement that people were no longer expected to be in the office for meetings. 'The most difficult situation previously was when you had a few people who were physically there for the meeting and others who were dialing in, because those present assumed the others hadn't bothered to get there,' says Rinsema.

Many meetings are now virtual, and communication takes place via web technology such as the company's Live Meeting service, using webcams and headsets. There are no fixed telephone lines in the building, and this has cut costs, increased efficiency and changed the way people communicate.

'Sixty-eight per cent of phone calls used to end in voicemail,' he says. 'Now, we see if someone is available by starting a chat conversation through [Microsoft] Communicator, then we can move into a voice conversation if necessary and we can bring other people into the conversation and use web cams to replace physical meetings.'

Although employees already had flexibility, they felt uncomfortable about using the 'working day' to do something different like playing tennis, shopping or spending time with their children. The move to the new building has gone along with explicit permission to do these things.

'You disconnect time from work,' says Been. 'Work is a series of activities to get results. You can meet or communicate smarter. You can save at least 20 per cent of your time or energy to do other things. You finally do those things that you said: "If only I had time I would do that". There is no excuse any more.'

This does not mean that it is easy to change people's habitual ways of thinking and working. As Been points out, teleworking has been around as a concept since the 1980s, and the technology is available and advancing all the time. Yet people still spend hours sitting in traffic jams on the way to work in offices. Attitudes have to be constantly challenged. 'It's we people who keep the patterns going.'

Human and carbon footprints

While some organizations are eagerly grasping the opportunities afforded by technology, others are finding themselves forced into change. Two factors are pushing them to cut space and to encourage remote working, says Professor Marmot, who is a leading expert on the design, management and use of places for work and learning.

The more immediate one is the high level of office rents, especially where space is constrained. The West End of London is the most expensive place in the world, with top quality office space costing as much as £120 per square foot at the end of 2010. 'Japan, Paris and New York are very expensive, but not compared with London,' she says. With average office occupancy rates at just over 50 percent during the working week, there is potential for 'huge savings' to be made.

The second, longer-term, factor is environmental sustainability. Organizations are under growing pressure to cut greenhouse gas emissions from their buildings. The UK, for example, is making the transition to a low carbon economy with a legally binding reduction in emissions of at least 80 percent by 2050. Penalties will rise over time for organizations that fail to comply.

The cost savings and environmental gains to be made by those who invest in green buildings can be substantial. **Macquarie Group**, a global financial services company based in Australia, has adopted 'activity-based' working at its new building in Shelley Street, Sydney, which was designed for collaboration and green benefits.

Everyone uses a laptop and the whole building is wireless, so people can choose the appropriate place for their changing needs during the day – from meeting rooms and themed 'breakout' areas to quiet zones, informal spaces for collaboration and cafés. Moving from Macquarie's previous office to Shelley Street led to a 52 percent reduction in paper use through printing and a 78 percent drop in paper storage space. The company says people also use elevators less, choosing to walk up and down the central staircase.

A culture change program accompanied the physical move, as Kate Strahorn, head of direct marketing for banking and financial services, told Australia's ABC National Radio. 'You're given a high degree of empowerment. But with that empowerment comes accountability, and with that accountability comes trust. So you really need to have those fundamentals with all of your people.'[7]

The **US federal government** is also promoting new ways of working as part of a drive to make its vast stock of real estate more efficient, cut costs and become a clean energy economy. The government is the largest property owner in the US, and President Obama has directed federal agencies to generate savings of $8bn by 2012 by eliminating excess building space and related spending.

While the agencies have telework policies, few employees have taken these up in the past because of management and cultural resistance and concerns about office cover. In 2008, less than 9 percent of the 1.2m eligible federal employees worked away from the office.[8]

Big change appears to be on the way, however. In 2010, Congress passed a bill to increase teleworking. Federal agencies are required to run training programs for employees and managers, designate senior managers to promote the policy and make it a core part of continuity planning. This could boost the number of teleworking employees to 1m, according to *Federal Times*, the online government news source.[9]

The General Services Administration, the agency responsible for federal buildings, is headed by Martha Johnson, an enthusiastic advocate of teleworking. The agency already had a major modernization project for its central office under way at the time of the telework legislation, and this provided a catalyst to explore how work gets done currently and to prepare for a new generation with different expectations and work styles.

In 2011, it embarked on a pilot for new approaches to work and management after 1200 agency staff moved to interim offices while their long-term home at 1800 F Street, Washington DC, was modernized. Three categories of employee began to emerge in the pilot: 'resident', or office-based, spending most of the day at their desk; 'roamers', who move around the site or campus but are rarely at their desks; and 'remote', working from home, on the move or at other sites, but rarely in the office.

The agency is exploring the redesign of its main office to accommodate about twice the number of employees that it does now, says Janet Pogue of

Gensler, the international architecture and design firm which is designing the new workplace.

'To achieve this, it will mean the building must support different activities,' she says. 'The reason people would come to the office would be very different. Employees would come in for face-to-face collaboration and group work that can't be done virtually, but not for individual focused work.'

The management implications are also being explored. Experience from the private sector suggests that senior executives and young employees are better at adapting to the new world of virtual work, while middle managers may find it more difficult, she says. 'Senior leaders have been mobile for years, traveling with their teams across the firm, but middle managers are used to seeing their staff face-to-face every day and they often have the greatest shift to make in managing people differently.'

However, managers have no choice but to adapt, Pogue believes. 'People in both the public and private sectors are realizing as they walk around their offices that most people are not at their desk any more. They are in meetings, traveling, with clients, or already working from home or a coffee shop down the street. Conference rooms are usually overbooked and no longer large enough. Work has clearly already shifted and it's time for the physical space to shift as well.'[10]

'In between' workspaces

As aging office buildings undergo refurbishment to make them more environmentally sustainable – known as 'green retrofitting' – a parallel trend is taking place with the rapid expansion of workspaces that offer mobile workers a halfway house between home and conventional offices.

These 'third spaces' cover a spectrum from formal serviced offices to private membership clubs to informal 'work hubs' and cafés that offer wireless internet access for the price of a cup of coffee. One example of a free third space is the **British Library** at St Pancras in London, which has become a popular drop-in place for focused work and meetings since it introduced WiFi and comfortable seating with power sockets for laptops.

The growing range of such 'in between' spaces provides variety and essential infrastructure for mobile employees and self-employed professionals with no fixed work abode other than home. While serviced offices can be very impersonal, some third spaces, such as clubs and business lounges, are trying to give nomadic workers a sense of belonging.

Commuting time is one of the biggest challenges around the world, as a report on the changing nature of work, *Agility @ Work*, underlines.

'In many developing economies, cities are becoming immobile – it can take hours to move around Beijing or Delhi,' say authors Mark Dixon, founder and chief executive of Regus, the leading provider of serviced offices, and Philip Ross, CEO of the Cordless Group, which specializes in the impact of technology on people, business and the built environment.

In Thailand, which has the world's longest commuting times, 37m hours are spent traveling to work every day, they say. 'In Bangkok, the average travel speed during the peak rush hour is now just seven miles per hour.'

Dixon and Ross believe there is a gap in the provision of places for people to work 'on the pause'. They predict a huge increase in third space, especially on the peripheries of cities, in transport hubs and in neighborhoods, which will help to reduce commuting and road congestion.

They also envisage corporate buildings having serviced offices or other spaces alongside them, run by external partners and providing additional meeting capacity, project areas and specialist technology such as videoconferencing when needed.

Technology is the catalyst and enabler of these future work trends, and management culture is the biggest hurdle, they say. 'But reducing the cost of real estate or "occupancy" will be seen to be a clear win-win, as new work styles change the cost base for doing business.'[11]

The nature of creativity

For organizations investing in buildings that respond to new work priorities, an important question is whether changes in the physical environment can make people more collaborative and creative.

A striking feature of new offices such as Microsoft's in Amsterdam and Macquarie's in Sydney is the emphasis on bright colors and light, airy spaces. Some companies in trend-conscious sectors such as technology and public relations go further, introducing as many unconventional features as possible in an effort to make work friendly, fun and collaborative.

At the London office of **Edelman**, the international PR firm, there is a café bar and a library of books and magazines right next to the entrance, and a cocktail bar on the way to the presentation rooms. While many employers would frown on social drinking in the workplace, Robert Phillips, CEO of Edelman in Europe, Middle East and Africa, believes it has its place. 'People start in a much more relaxed way in the bar and then go into a presentation and you've broken down the barriers.' Phillips says one of his principles of leadership is to create a culture of collaboration and creativity in the wider sense, 'and that is why today's leaders have to properly consider the physical environment in which their people work'.[12]

Google, the world's leading internet company, is famous for the free meals, casual dress, pool tables and colorful deckchairs on display at its offices. The engineers can take time out of their main job to develop new business ideas, a freedom that has generated some of the search engine's biggest innovations. 'It's much less about top-down structure and processes than at a traditional organization,' says Matt Brittin, CEO of Google in the UK and Ireland.[13]

In some respects, though, working practices are fairly conventional. Engineers and sales people sit in long rows in the open-plan London 'GooglePlex', absorbed in their PCs and Macs, or chatting in small groups. It's still a predominantly young workforce, with many employees in their mid-20s to early 30s. The perks and quirks – party balloons, rubber ducks stuck upside down on the ceiling, sweets, salads and drinks on tap – seem geared to keep people in the office, something that Brittin acknowledges. 'Our business is built on collaboration,' he says. 'You can work flexibly and from home but it's not encouraged on a continuous basis.'

As for creativity, Brittin says he gets his best ideas while cycling to work through the peaceful surroundings of London's Richmond Park. 'It's just me and my bike and the occasional deer,' he said in a *Financial Times* interview.[14]

Can the physical look and feel of an office really make a difference to people's level of creativity? Professor Marmot of University College London is doubtful.

'We know that people say they are most creative and thoughtful when in natural environments with views of trees, mountains, lakes or seas. It's never at their desk at home or in the office,' she says. 'If you're interested in effective work in the knowledge economy, ideas generation and knowledge sharing, it cannot be fostered through space design, but through rewarding thought.

'Google for example has done lots of groovy things such as meetings in a rowing boat or in a bath or round a beehive, as if shaking up the physical environment might help do things better. I'm not sure we can say that's the case. The kooky thing doesn't make you creative, it just makes a statement that you're in the IT industry with a brand that's young and trendy. When you see how people actually work in those industries, it's not necessarily very different.'

Marmot argues that creativity can be hindered by dirty, uninspiring physical surroundings and by not having the right equipment in the right place. 'But you can't necessarily help creativity just by doing the office environment well.'

Breaking down resistance

Collaboration is an important theme in the sparkling new **Unilever** offices in Hamburg's huge HafenCity development zone. The views over the River Elbe are a big break with the past for employees of the consumer goods company in the north German industrial city. The award-winning building, completed in 2009, is designed to be environmentally sustainable and transparent, with a café, grocery store and spa to attract the public and serve employees.

The move from an 18-storey building in another part of Hamburg was also motivated by the war for talent, says Harry Brouwer, the group's chairman for Germany, Austria and Switzerland. 'If you want top people you have to have top premises. The number of people who want to join Unilever increased significantly since we moved into the new building and actively updated the company culture.'[15]

The old Hamburg building had individual offices and long dark corridors and there was little interaction between people and departments. In the new Unilever Haus, people can work anywhere, including the roof terrace, with wireless connection to the local area network. The interior is entirely open-plan, with no walled rooms and doors, even for the leadership team.

Two weeks after they moved in, a veteran employee told Brouwer that she had seen more of him in the short time in the new building than she had seen of the board of directors in the previous 20 years.

The exterior resembles an ocean liner, which is appropriate since the building is a flagship for Unilever's company-wide 'agile working' strategy. Personal offices, including those for senior leaders, are being consigned to history. New buildings and renovations are being designed for better communication and to accommodate 30–50 percent higher densities of people, enabling significant cost savings on real estate, the company says. They will be equipped with advanced teleconferencing facilities, 'free address' workstations that anyone can use, soft phones that make calls from a computer via the Internet rather than a fixed line, and 'thin client devices', which are mobile terminals that draw their computational power from central servers.

'Anytime anywhere', as practiced by Microsoft and many other technology companies, was an unfamiliar concept to most of Unilever's people in Hamburg. Not everyone yet has the tools to work remotely, and the 1100 managers and staff have to get used to performance measurement based on output not hours. 'We're starting the process,' says Brouwer.

To encourage greater autonomy and initiative, he has introduced what he calls the 'one-metre rule', which states that employees should deal with issues arising in their sphere of responsibility without asking permission of their manager. 'People appreciate this, but they are not used to it and still feel a bit insecure about it.'

There are ongoing discussions with the top 50 executives about managing people in the new environment. 'We talk about agile working, how to deal with the workforce, and leadership development. We talk openly about trust and coping with the fear of losing control of people. This is something you have to deal with. If someone isn't there, what does it mean? Does it mean loss of control, or better output?'

To help managers confront their fears, the leadership team invited a blind mountain-climber to come and talk about what it was like to experience every single move as a step into the unknown. 'We were saying to them: You too can move out of your zone of comfort.'

Like Theo Rinsema at Microsoft, Brouwer had to go through his own evolution 'from control to letting go', which he did in his previous role as head of the Benelux region of Unilever. In his current job, he works one day a week from his home office in Holland. Other members of the senior team telecommute, but still only occasionally.

'There is quite a lot of discussion and insecurity about working away from the office because people aren't used to it,' Brouwer says. 'The younger generation don't have a problem with it, but the challenge is to get the older generation to do this because they are used to working at specific desks.'

The transition is work in progress. But employee engagement, measured through Unilever's global 'pulse survey', has risen strongly since the move to the new building and the changes taking place in the internal culture.

New rules for the new world

If hands-off management is the new order of the day, rules might seem out of place. In fact, the new world of work needs new rules to help people to break out of old habits and ensure they adopt the new ones. These rules are unlikely to look or sound much like the old ones, although how they are expressed will depend on the type of organization you work for.

Vodafone's UK headquarters was redesigned when CEO Guy Laurence took over in early 2009. Laurence had previously led a recovery of the mobile operator's business in the Netherlands, where a similar switch from closed to open-plan offices was a key ingredient. 'We always start with the physical environment,' he says. 'That changes the way you are able to manage people.'

The atmosphere at the UK offices, on a purpose-built campus near Newbury, west of London, is informal, with most of the 4500 staff including Laurence wearing casual gear. There are no individual offices and all meetings of six or fewer people take place in the ground-floor café area, so 'we can grab people as they walk past'.

Laurence says he expects people to use common sense. But there are strict rules about the space and how it is used:

- Open-plan means just that. If anyone moves filing cabinets around their desk to create some privacy, 'they get a phone call from me saying "I suggest you don't do that" '.

- No one, including the CEO, has more than a single drawer in a filing cabinet to keep their possessions.

- When people move desk or building they have to carry their own belongings. This is to prevent clutter and paper files. 'Everything is electronically archived'.

- There are £50 fines for talking in the three glass-enclosed rooms available for silent, concentrated work. These 'libraries' are shared, spacious rooms. Previously, they had tried small booths for concentrated work but abandoned them 'because people turned them into private offices'.

- New recruits have to travel to meet colleagues face-to-face when they first join. Once accomplished, they are discouraged from traveling, and have to communicate electronically instead. This has cut business miles and business flights by more than a quarter.

Microsoft Netherlands also has a set of rules for behavior in its Amsterdam office:

- People cannot take up residence of a space and then wander off, leaving their belongings. 'Camping forbidden' signs enforce the policy. 'If you don't use your place for two hours, you have to clean it and leave', says Gonnie Been.

- To make meetings more productive, every team agrees a 'physical minimum' – how much it needs to meet in person to be able to collaborate virtually in the most effective way. For example, the Netherlands management team meets in person for a day and a half every quarter but holds its monthly three-hour meetings virtually, with people logging in from different fixed locations (calling from a car is not allowed).

- There are also generic rules for meetings. 'You have to read the documents beforehand, and there are no exceptions,' Been says. 'If you want something on the agenda, it has to be there 48 hours beforehand, including all documents for preparation. At one meeting, nobody put any items on the agenda, so the meeting was cancelled.'

We give further guidance in Chapter 9 on how to deal with the vexed issue of meetings in future work.

Next generation

Adapting to a world of work defined by trust, freedom and responsibility should in theory be easier for young people starting their careers, because they are not caught up in old habits. Yet this next generation, too, arrives with a set of assumptions.

When Microsoft invited a group of 16–20 year olds to visit the new Amsterdam building, their questions revealed both apprehension and excitement about the possibilities. 'Do people *work* here?' they asked incredulously. 'Is work fun?' 'Who is controlling you?' 'Where is your boss?'

In summary

The conventional office is not well-suited to a world in which a growing proportion of work can be done anywhere, at any time. Offices of the future, whether corporate buildings or 'third spaces' between office and home, will be primarily meeting places that also accommodate concentrated work, rather than the other way round. Emerging office models are based on principles of:

- Transparency
- Sustainability
- Interconnectedness
- Collaboration
- Personal responsibility

Office layout and design can convey important messages about transparency, collaboration and individual responsibility, and they can help people to realize their potential. Yet even a radical change in physical environment will not be enough without an accompanying shift in organizational culture and leadership style. To achieve this, leaders and managers need to:

- Confront their fears
- Move from control to trust
- Separate status from hierarchy
- Be visible, physically or virtually
- Encourage initiative and accountability
- Make balance a priority

In Chapter 7, we explore culture. Based on our research findings, we discover what kind of organizational culture is needed to make a successful shift to future work. We also explore how countries and regions of the world differ in their openness to the changes that are under way.

CHAPTER 7

Culture is critical

> *The entire knowledge economy is built on the trust that employees and their employers have in each other; there really is nothing else. It is only this relationship – the one between the employees and the organization – that keeps a company going.*
>
> Vineet Nayar, CEO, HCL Technologies[1]

We have talked about leadership and culture change as being essential if organizations are to seize the competitive advantages offered by new ways of working. The findings of our specially designed survey, described below, reveal the type of organizational culture that will adapt most easily to the forces transforming work. However, the managers we questioned reported a big gap between current organizational cultures and what they view as the ideal culture for the new world of work.

National cultures also play an important part in determining how easily future work styles will spread, an issue we address in the second part of the chapter. Although there are big differences between regions and countries, it would be a mistake to regard people's desire for greater choice and control of their working lives as a concern only in advanced economies. Companies doing business around the globe need to understand how attitudes and expectations are also changing in the growing markets from which they will increasingly draw talent.

Part one: organizational cultures

What managers say

Organizations that have already implemented future work models have many common features. Their management style is often distinctly different from the traditional top-down, control-oriented corporate regimes that held sway during the twentieth century. But what exactly is it that makes the difference? Why do people feel more motivated and productive in some organizations than others? What are the links between successful management practices of the twenty-first century and innovative ways of working?

To answer these questions, we turned to the people who face these issues daily – managers from around the world. With the help of two business schools, Cass and Henley, we obtained responses from 366 managers to an in-depth survey about them and the organizations for which they work.

About half our respondents were based in the UK. The rest represented 38 nationalities working in 40 countries. As well as the alumni of Cass and Henley, about 120 responses came from managers around the world through our various networks.

Key survey findings:

■ Two-thirds of managers believe there will be a revolution in working practices in the next decade

■ Most feel their organizations are not adapting quickly enough to new ways of working

■ Nearly 90 percent believe people are more productive given autonomy over their working patterns

■ Over 80 percent think new ways of working would benefit the business and nearly 60 percent want more freedom to let people work flexibly

■ Women put a higher priority than men on giving people freedom to achieve results in their own way

■ Organizations that encourage new work styles, such as remote working, are much more likely than others to value creativity, to trust employees and to assume they are self-motivated

■ These types of organization are much closer to what managers say is their ideal culture

Actual versus ideal cultures

We asked a series of questions about the values, management style, processes and decision-making they experience in their current organization and then asked them what they would like to see in an ideal situation. We expected some differences between reality and the ideal, but were surprised to find the size of gap that emerged.

Underlying every organization there is a set of values. In some, these values are expressed openly, clearly set out in mission statements and repeated in public proclamations. In others they are not explicitly stated and have to be deduced from management behavior.

In many cases, values expressed publicly at the top are at odds with the actual behavior in the organization. Senior managers set the tone. If they work extreme hours, they send a message that success is associated with complete dedication to the job, at the expense of personal life. They may say they support flexible working, but their behavior is what will be believed. They may say that they reward people for results, but if in practice they are seen to favor people who are visibly putting in lots of time in the office or on late night emails, then that becomes the cultural norm.

We, therefore, set out to discover what managers currently experience and how this compares with what they believe the culture should be like. We asked them to rate their organization on a scale between two opposite statements, A and B, where A represented a traditional approach and B represented the characteristics we believed were conducive to future work.

We use 'Type A' and 'Type B' as shorthand for two distinct types of organizational culture. In common with Douglas McGregor's 'Theory X' and 'Theory Y', the management practices are based on opposite assumptions. Type A organizations have a 'command and control' style of management, monitoring people closely because they cannot be trusted to work on their own. Type B organizations, on the other hand, give responsibility to employees, empowering them to make decisions for themselves and trusting them to get on with the job.

In total, we asked questions about 25 pairs of opposite management styles to cover a broad range of elements of organizational culture. These are listed in **Figure 7.1**. We asked managers to answer the same 25 questions about their current organization and then about their ideal one. The difference between the two answers showed us how well employers were meeting the hopes and expectations of their managers.

We found that for every one of the 25 factors, managers rated their current organization closer to A than they would like it to be. Top of the list, with the highest gap between the actual and ideal culture was 'A = Multi-level sign-off' and 'B = Freedom to act'. In this case, two-thirds of respondents described their current organization as A, while only a quarter chose B. However, when asked what they believed was the most effective approach to management, only 15 percent chose A, while over 70 percent opted for B.

So, based on this answer, about half of the managers in the survey are currently working in a Type A culture but would prefer a Type B. They see their current organization as keeping decision-making power at too high a level and not delegating authority or freedom to get on with the job.

This is also evident in the second most misaligned factor: 'A = Follow the rules' versus 'B = Question the rules'. It appears that many organizations

TYPE A	TYPE B
Organizational Values	
People seen as a disposable resource	People seen as a long-term investment
People status conscious, hierarchical	All people are equal
People are closely monitored	People take responsibility
Keep personal life separate	Work and personal life intertwined
Work is serious	Work is fun
People need to be directed	People are self-motivated
Management Style	
Bureaucratic, formal	Casual, informal
'Do what I tell you'	'Do the right thing'
Competitive (between employees)	Collaborative teamwork
Cut back on cost	Improve effectiveness/productivity
Short-term focus	Long-term focus
Low trust in employees	High trust in employees
Rigid	Flexible
Management Processes	
Manager-only appraisal	360-degree appraisal
Individual performance pay	Team/Organization-based pay
Multi-level hierarchy	Flat structure
Necessary information only	Open communications
Command and control	Enable and empower
Reward time/attendance	Reward outcomes/targets
Keep work in-house	Outsource where possible
Decision-Making	
Top-down decisions	Everyone has a vote
Managers decide	Teams decide
Follow precedent	Be creative
Multi-level sign-off	Freedom to act
Follow the rules	Question the rules

Figure 7.1 Type A and Type B Cultures

expect people to blindly do what they are told and not to use their initiative. Yet managers know that this is not the best way of engaging their employees.

When asked about 'A = Follow Precedent' versus 'B = Be Creative', almost half of managers put their organization in A but only 7 percent thought this was ideal. It appears that the way to get on in those cultures is to keep a low profile and not come up with new ideas. Yet managers clearly believe that the best way to run an enterprise is to tap into the creativity of their people.

Similar numbers say that their current organizations work on 'necessary information only' while they would overwhelmingly prefer 'open communications'. They strongly believe that employers should focus on individual effectiveness and productivity, as opposed to cutting costs, yet in practice only half do so. Two-thirds work in a status-conscious culture, yet the same proportion believe all people should be treated equally. The main results of the survey are detailed in **Appendix 1**.

Tackling inertia

These results show that there is a major mismatch between what is actually happening and what managers would prefer. But if these are the managers who are running teams and operations in those businesses, why are they not practicing what they believe? What is stopping them from managing in a more effective and empowering way? We think that inertia is standing in the way of change. The attitude often seems to be that, unless there is a serious crisis, there is no need to change the existing way of getting things done.

Many senior managers have built their careers and credibility on a lifetime of working in a particular way. If it was good enough to get them to the top, then it's good enough for the next generation, they say. This was underlined by the answer to a question in the second part of our survey.

We asked respondents to agree or disagree with the following statement: 'Senior managers think that the way they have always worked is the right one'. Half of them agreed, or strongly agreed with the statement, while 34 percent disagreed or strongly disagreed.

As we have seen from the examples throughout this book, support from the top is essential to success. In some innovative companies like W L Gore or Google or Semco in Brazil, the founders set the tone, while in others, such as BDO or Gap or Microsoft Netherlands, leaders with vision have set about changing the culture and ways of working. Shifting management habits in a large organization is almost impossible without a champion for the cause who has the influence to make the change happen.

However, as the bottom line benefits become increasingly obvious, we believe resistance will be harder to maintain. Future work will no longer be confined to a few interesting companies but will be commonly accepted as a sensible way of getting the best return from an employer's most important asset. This view seems to be shared by the managers who responded to our survey. Their reaction to the statement 'There will be a revolution in working practices in the next decade' was emphatic. Two-thirds agreed and only 16 percent disagreed.

Cisco's collaborative leadership model

Cisco, which has a largely mobile workforce, operates what it calls a 'collaborative leadership model'. This incorporates many of the characteristics of a Type B organization outlined above.

Marilyn Nagel, chief diversity officer for the networking equipment company, explains how it came about. 'We moved from a standard command-and-control situation where we had traditional functional lines of business directed by the person at the top,' she says. 'There wasn't enough cross-functional collaboration and that led to a lack of diversity of thought, to groupthink and negative dynamics.'

There has been a boost to innovation from having more perspectives than before, when people were operating in functional silos. 'For example, instead of there being one head of engineering as there was, there's an engineering council made up of a variety of leaders within the engineering organization. People come together very quickly for a project with less focus on "what's the hierarchy?" and more on "what do we really need in this area to get it done quickly?"'

Not surprisingly, Cisco makes extensive use of new work styles, with 85 percent of employees teleworking. 'We're independent regarding location and substantially in control of our work schedules.'

The model requires the technological tools for collaboration and also a change in attitudes, Nagel says. 'You have to have a workforce and leadership team that's willing to look at leaders of the future, not just today and of the past. It's the new work world. The Millennial generation works like this very easily.'

Companies often need a lever to begin the transition to future work. In Cisco's case, the levers have been its own technology and the way that the next generation communicates. 'Our leaders often refer to how their children are using Skype,' says James Brooks, director, employee engagement, and leader of Cisco's flexible work initiatives.

He notes, however, that change does not come easily. 'The challenges are tradition and familiarity. Marilyn and I are both psychologists. We know the challenges of getting people to change, especially someone who has been working in a particular way a long time and has been successful. The leader really needs to "get it". It takes some imagination to go there.'

Linking culture to future work

How exactly does organizational culture relate to the adoption of future work practices? We wanted to see if there was any link between these practices and Type A versus Type B cultures. We asked survey respondents about the flexible working practices in their businesses. We then divided the responses into those from 'High' Type B organizations (those displaying more than 10 of the 25 factors categorized as B) versus the rest.

We found that cultures that were predominantly Type B were much more likely to have people working from home. About half of them had home-based workers compared to only a third of other employers. They were also more likely to have mobile workers, term time-only workers, part-time working, compressed hours and hot-desking.

So, the findings bore out our observations about cultures that support flexible working. To check this further, we looked at respondents' answers to the statement: 'My organization encourages new ways of working'. We split them into those who agreed, or strongly agreed, with this statement ('pro' organizations) and those who disagreed, or strongly disagreed ('anti' organizations).

Not surprisingly, only 26 percent of the 'anti' employers were rated as flexible, versus 73 percent of the 'pro' ones. More importantly, we found that employers that encourage new ways of working are three times more likely to enable and empower their people generally than 'anti' ones. They are also much more likely to value creativity, trust employees, assume they are self-motivated and allow them to 'do the right thing'. As many as 84 percent of the 'pro' organizations reward outcomes and targets rather than time and attendance, compared with only 44 percent of the 'anti' ones.

It is clear from our survey, as well as our observations of leading organizations, that there is a type of culture that is associated with future work. This Type B culture is much more open to implementing new working practices because its existing values and processes will support the necessary changes.

Looked at another way, those organizations that have adopted new working practices are most likely to have a culture of trust and empowerment. To erase any doubt about the importance of empowerment, a massive 95 percent of the managers in our survey agreed with the statement that 'Good leadership is about empowering people'. This brings us firmly to the conclusion that the adoption of future work practices is a strong indicator of good leadership and a progressive organizational culture.

Gender and leadership styles

Type B cultures are more people-oriented than Type A's. They consider people to be a long-term investment rather than a disposable asset. They expect them to work collaboratively in an environment of open communication. They give people freedom to act on their own initiative. This contrasts with the traditional command-and-control, hierarchical structures that were designed and built for an era when the vast majority of the workforce, and all of those at the top, were male.

Type B cultures contain characteristics often associated with a more 'female' style of leadership and management – one that motivates people, builds effective teams, fosters trust and respect and takes into account the wider world. Research studies have identified such characteristics as important leadership attributes for the twenty-first century, as well as ones in which women do particularly well.[2]

Interest in gender-balanced leadership has been heightened by the financial and economic crisis. As the book *Why Women Mean Business* puts it: 'The need for countries and companies to make best use of women's potential in addressing the challenges of the 21st century is even more urgent today. It is only through the leadership of women *and* men, working as partners, that we can build a saner, safer and more sustainable model of capitalism.'[3]

In our survey, we had responses from 225 men and 141 women, giving us a reasonable sample to analyze further. On average, the women rated their current organizations as slightly less Type A and more Type B than the men. The fact that their environment is already more B could be due to their direct influence on the management style or it could be that they chose to work in this type of culture. Slightly more women than men agreed that their organization encouraged new ways of working and that it did its best to improve the work–life balance of its people. Just over half the men and 69 percent of the women said they worked in a high trust environment.

Gender differences were more pronounced in the ratings for the ideal organization. Women showed a stronger belief in 360-degree appraisal, open communications, improved effectiveness and collaborative teamwork. Eighty percent of women opted to question the rules rather than follow them, compared with 68 percent of the men. Ninety-one percent said they would like their people to be creative and not just follow precedent, compared with 81 percent of the men.

So the women in our survey feel more strongly than the men about creating an environment in which individuals have freedom to work in their own way to achieve results. They were also nearly ten percent more inclined than men to want people to do the right thing rather than do what they were told.

Interestingly, the women who responded to the survey were happier with their own personal flexibility than the men. Only 49 percent said they would like more control over where, when and how they do their job, compared with 59 percent of the men. This may reflect the fact that men often face greater resistance – and more perceived career damage – when asking their employer for greater choice and control over their working arrangements than women do. This is something that companies need to rectify. If they base their talent management strategies on the assumption that women are the only ones who want flexibility, they are seriously out of date.

As one of us wrote in an article in *The Conference Board Review*: 'Organizations that want to promote gender diversity in their top ranks need to understand what's happening to a growing proportion of men in their workforce. Instead of continuing to focus all their gender-diversity efforts on women, companies would do better to take account of the other side of the coin. Enabling men to play their full role as fathers is good not only for children and families but also for women's progress in the workplace and for developing more rounded leaders of both genders.'[4]

Part two: national cultures

Future work around the world

Work cultures vary widely around the world. Social attitudes and expectations, communications infrastructure, legislation and public policy can all affect a country's openness to new work styles. Executives we interviewed for this book stressed the need for cultural sensitivity when implementing a future work program.

Working from home is a case in point. While increasingly common in countries like the US and UK, it is far from being globally practical. 'In many cultures, people don't have an office at home, or the space and quiet atmosphere to work, so it's not feasible,' says Helen Wyatt, a senior HR executive at Unilever. 'There are also legal, insurance and safety issues about remote working in different countries, so the ability to do this is patchy.'[5]

Thomson Reuters, the information group, collected interesting data on country differences when introducing flexible working guidelines across its content, technology and operations (CT&O) division. The division employs about 9000 people in operational centers in China, India, Thailand, the Philippines and Poland, as well as in head offices in the US and UK.

It found that working from home is an option in most places, but can be a challenge in some parts of Asia where internet connections are unreliable, slow and expensive, there are sometimes power outages and many employees live with their families around them. Job-sharing can be an issue in countries where local employment laws and regulations do not recognize the status of such workers, and there are cultural barriers, as sharing a role is a completely new concept.

In Asia, people value salary, career advancement, competitive benefits and convenient work locations more highly than flexible work, says Sarah Cavanagh, global head of HR for the division. Despite this, managers in the operational centers welcomed the idea of flexible work as positive for employee engagement and retention.

'The place where we had the most difficulty was the US because there was a real culture of presenteeism,' says Cavanagh. A year on, however, most employees in London and New York are able to work from home if they want to without seeking permission. 'The culture was already flexible in the UK, and there's been a change of mindset in North America. We work in a global organization, communicating with teams in different time zones, so virtual and home working are necessities to do the job.'[6]

Among advanced economies, the UK is furthest ahead in its range of work flexibility, according to Caroline Waters, director of people and policy at BT, the communications group. 'America has made significant advances but I don't think they have such a sophisticated model,' she says. 'In Germany, the tax legislation is prohibitive, although lately more examples are emerging. Works councils have some concerns but continue to be a part of the debate.

'France hasn't had great take-up nationally but again there are pockets of good practice. In France, the unions have tended to focus on the length of the working week rather than when and how people want to work. Again, the good news is that this is changing as the possibilities presented by greater flexibility become more widely understood. In countries such as Italy and the Czech Republic, BT's flexible workers are seen as "trend-setters".'[7]

A useful guide to this global cultural maze, *Balancing Work and Family*,[8] looks at the availability and use of a wide range of approaches, including flexible hours, flexible location and flexible careers. In Kenya and Nigeria, for example, human resources managers view telecommuting and alternative work schedules with suspicion and mistrust, and poor infrastructure and lack of access to technology are barriers to new ways of working. In Latin America, the book says, young people moving into management roles in the next decade are seen as catalysts for change. They have a different attitude to work, 'having seen their parents and other lifetime employees suddenly become unemployed because of mergers or restructuring'.

Professor Nuria Chinchilla, co-editor of the book and director of the International Center for Work and Family at IESE Business School in Barcelona, says relationships at work, in the family and in society are changing everywhere, especially with the mass entry of women into the labor market. 'Companies doing business around the world must respond to pressure to create fairer, more human working environments which are also more productive and competitive,' she says.

Europe is grappling with aging populations and low birth rates. Talent is at a premium, and there is also a strong focus in many countries on reconciling careers and family life. Working patterns and hours vary widely across the region, from an average of nearly 43 hours per week in Greece to below 31 hours in the Netherlands.[9] Part-time work is uncommon in eastern and southern Europe but it is widely practiced in some northern countries such as Sweden, Germany, the UK and Denmark.[10]

The Netherlands is a particularly striking example of how attitudes to working hours and location are changing, with the rise of dual-income couples and greater sharing of family responsibilities between women and men.

Rise of the Dutch 'daddy day'

The Dutch are 'world champions' of part-time work, says Professor Paul Schnabel, director of The Netherlands Institute for Social Research. Over three-quarters of Dutch women work reduced hours, compared with a European Union average of 32 percent. In recent years, however, there has been a big rise in the number of men working a four-day week, or working from home once a week, to look after the children, an arrangement known as *papadag* ('daddy day').

Over a third of Dutch men now work a shorter week, according to the institute. Of these, 25 percent have part-time jobs, against an EU average of just 8 percent. The rest fit a full-time job into four long days, or spend short days at work and make up the shortfall during evenings and weekends.

Employers generally accept this. 'I'm an employer myself and it's quite a normal thing,' says Prof Schnabel. 'If people apply for a job, we ask them whether they would like to do four days or five days. I'm not in favor of people working long hours because you become less productive if you work nine or ten hours.'[11]

For employers, it is a way to attract and keep good people. 'Once the recession is over, the job market is going to be very tight,' says Ronald van de Krol, editor of the Saturday edition of *Het Financieele Dagblad*, the leading daily financial newspaper, who works in the office four days a week and spends one 'daddy day' at home. 'Younger managers in their 30s and 40s have grown up with people around them working four days. So it's not strange for a man to say "I'll take the job, and I want to work four days or work a day from home".'[12]

Employees have to be flexible, however. 'For the employer, it works really well because the employee tends to do the same amount of work for less money,' says van de Krol. 'You continue to work, even when you're not *at* work. It requires a level of trust by the employer. But people say they get a lot more done at home if they have to write a report, for example, because there are fewer interruptions.'

The trend aligns with the Dutch government's drive to encourage people to work more frequently from home to reduce road congestion and costly office space. It also reflects national attitudes. 'If you ask a Dutch person whether they want more time or more money, they almost always go for more time,' he says.

Legislation introduced in 2000 gives all employees the right to reduced hours, as in Belgium, France and Germany, unless the employer can show a serious business or safety reason why this is not possible.[13] The extensive use of reduced hours is also due to primary schools being closed on Wednesday afternoons, and to Dutch society frowning on parents who put their children in childcare for five days a week. Half of all women work fewer than 25 hours a week.[14] The traditional female part-time model has been coming under pressure, however, with a government taskforce calling for women to increase their hours to at least 25 a week to ease labor shortages.

Although arguably progressive, the Dutch approach is still largely a variation on the traditional work model. People work a set number of hours and days, rather than being measured and rewarded purely on output.

Technology leads the way

In some countries, it is the fast pace of technological development that is forcing a rethink of how and where work is done. South Korea is a prime example of this. In 2010, the government announced an ambitious 'smart work initiative' to have 30 percent of employees working from home, on the move or from specially equipped 'smart work' centers by 2015, using laptops and mobile internet devices.[15] The capital, Seoul, is a world leader in high-speed broadband connections.

The new policy, designed to improve productivity and cut congestion and carbon emissions, represents a dramatic shift from a work culture heavily reliant on face-time in the office. South Korea has among the longest working hours of any OECD country, at an average of 47 hours per week, with relatively low labor productivity levels.[16]

Employers' and employees' willingness to change will be a decisive factor. However, if successful, the strategy could boost low female participation in the labor force and the extremely low birth rate of 1.15 by enabling more women to combine career and family by working from, or near, their homes. Research shows that countries that make it easier for parents to continue working tend to see higher birth rates and higher growth through greater female participation in the labor force.[17]

Common ground

In our survey of managers around the world, the UK respondents rated both their actual and ideal organizations as being closer to Type B than respondents from other countries. Most notably, almost half the UK managers classified their actual organization as encouraging creativity, compared with only a third of respondents from the rest of the world.

However, all the respondents agreed that their current organizations should ideally be significantly more Type B than they are. Since most were alumni of two UK-based business schools, this uniformity is perhaps not surprising.

Asked what would be most effective, over 80 percent of all the managers opted for creativity over compliance. Two-thirds of non-UK managers, and 77 percent of UK managers, also opted for 'question the rules' versus 'follow the rules' for their ideal organization.

Overall our conclusion is that the UK is marginally more inclined toward Type B organizational cultures, but there is a highly consistent view around the world about the desire to shift from Type A to Type B.

Another indication of common ground comes from a survey of employee engagement by BlessingWhite, an international consulting firm, covering North America, Europe, Australia and New Zealand, South East Asia, India and China.[18] Covering 11,000 employees, it asked people to choose the item that would most improve their job satisfaction.

'Career development opportunities and training' and 'More opportunities to do what I do best' were the first two in every region, except in SE Asia where 'More flexible job conditions (eg. control over how my work gets done, flex time, etc)' came second. Flexible conditions came third in Europe, North America and Australia, fourth in China and fifth in India. So greater control over how work is done has a universal appeal. In all cases it beat 'Improved cooperation among my co-workers' and 'A better relationship with my manager'.

Talent in the global economy

Multinational companies, competing for talent around the world, can gain by innovating in this area. Here we look at two examples in India, where the need to attract and retain able, skilled people is forcing a review of traditional work and career models.

HSBC, one of the largest banking groups in the world, introduced flexible work options in India in 2008 in response to an employee survey showing that 'work–life balance' was a concern. Nikunj Upadhyay, vice-president for organizational development at HSBC in Mumbai, says it was the first foreign bank in India to do so. Flexible work, once only available in the IT sector, is now becoming more widely accepted by multinationals in India as a way to attract and keep diverse talent.

'People are looking to have greater control and a more balanced life,' she says. 'In the past, these things were not so important to employees. But Indian society has changed and so have people's expectations. For the newer generations in the workforce, Gen X and Gen Y, flexibility has become a priority.'[19]

About 10 percent of HSBC's 6500 employees in India have formally opted for the program, most of them varying their start and finish times where previously they had to get to the office by 8.30 a.m. each day. This has cut hours of commuting and given them more time for personal needs.

It takes time to break old habits and address managerial concerns, she says. But the culture is becoming more flexible and managers are getting better at encouraging people to find the right option for themselves. The aim is that people should be measured on outcomes not hours. 'We're working towards a results-only environment. We position this as a better way to do business because it enhances your productivity at work. We're not completely there, but the mindset is changing.'

HSBC India, which is chaired by a woman, Naina Lal Kidwai, has invested heavily in technology to enable some people to work from home with secure electronic access to the office. In a telework pilot, one of the bank's sales teams increased productivity and exceeded its sales targets. Regular teleworking is still rare, however. 'Sometimes the nature of the role may not favor telecommuting if it's heavily dependent on systems which need the individual to be in the designated workplace,' says Ms Upadhyay.

Mayur Singh, a senior vice-president in the Risk function, is a prime example of the bank's changing approach to work and careers. Each year, he spends six months in the Mumbai office and six months doing ecological restoration and community outreach at Kemri Conservation, a project in the northern state of Rajasthan to which he is deeply committed.

'The Kemri project is tremendously enriching as a personal development opportunity and very fulfilling from a social contribution perspective,' says Singh, who is in his 40s. 'It provides teamwork and leadership experience in a rural environment, working with diverse people outside the usual comfort zone of a corporate office.'

The arrangement is an effective retention tool and contributes significantly to his sense of engagement with HSBC, he says. 'Each year when I resume work on 1st April, the bank has found suitable senior leadership roles for me, usually short-term projects as these become available because the bank has significant growth plans in India.'

Another company trying to address the changing attitudes of employees in India is **Deloitte**, the professional services firm, which has introduced a tool to help them define their own 'career-life fit'. The tool, known as Mass Career Customization (MCC), was first applied to Deloitte's US practice. It describes careers in terms of a corporate 'lattice', rather than a corporate ladder, offering employees options to change the pace of their job, workload, location and schedule, and type of role at different stages in their working lives.

The firm decided to introduce MCC in India to attract talent, give young people in particular a new reason to stay and inspire performance, says Bob

Chapman, managing partner of Deloitte's India operation. In growing numbers of Indian families, both spouses have careers and are equally involved in raising children. 'We also wanted our US and India professionals working as a single integrated team.'[20]

Deloitte's new approach is still work in progress. The firm employs about 10,000 people in Hyderabad, Mumbai and Bangalore. Eighteen months after introducing the options, only just over one percent had actually chosen to accelerate or decelerate their career, although all are eligible to do so. Chapman says the concept is relatively new to the Indian workforce and to the firm as a whole, and 'we are continuously educating our people and raising awareness on MCC and career-life fit'. He adds that the goal is not to 'sell' formal flexibility but to help provide staff with options as their needs change.

How managers can prepare

In our survey, we wanted to find out what managers had experienced in the way of preparation and training to manage people in the new world of work. Regardless of age, a large majority felt they had the right skills to manage teams working remotely or flexibly. However, just over half of managers aged 40-plus, and two-thirds of those under 40, said they had 'never been trained to manage remote/flexible employees'.

Managing such employees will increasingly be the norm. As the case studies in this book demonstrate, the successful introduction of future work practices often depends on a change in organizational culture. Managers will almost certainly need help with this process, as much as with the practicalities of implementing new work styles. In the most compelling examples we have seen, senior leaders recognize the need to change their own behavior and organizations run programs to address managerial resistance and inertia and to improve key skills such as open and consistent communication with employees.

In Chapters 8 and 9, we offer a guide to making this culture change happen, demonstrating how businesses large and small are learning in practical terms to adapt and thrive in the new world of work.

CHAPTER 8

How to break free of the old model

Laura Terheyden is in her late 20s and works in San Francisco. Like many of her peers in Generation Y – young people now entering, or already in, the workforce – she places a high value on anything an employer can do to make life easier as she focuses on building her career. Being able to decide where and when she works is a big part of that.

Speaking at a conference panel on generations in the workplace, she told the audience her own work style was worlds apart from that of peers in other companies. 'Some of my friends are amazed when they hear about the flexibility I have,' she said. 'A lot of my friends work in places where they feel like they are clocking in and clocking out even as salaried employees. That's a struggle for them. One of them, who is in a finance function, has to stay in her cube and her comings and goings are watched by an older member of staff.' [1]

Her friend feels under pressure to tell her boss when she is not at her work-station, for example when going to lunch or leaving for the day. 'The older co-worker, to whom she does not report, expects my friend to be physically present on a routine schedule that matches her own, even though my friend may be working after hours at home or on weekends unbeknownst to her colleague.'

By contrast, Laura enjoys what she calls a 'flexible workspace', with the freedom to work outside the confines of specified time and place. She is part of the diversity and inclusion team at McKesson, the US healthcare company. 'Instead of working 9–5 in an office or designated cube, I may work from home, a coffee shop, a park with Wi-Fi, or have a cube-share with another employee. I work the amount of hours needed to get the job done by the deadline instead of doing the job between certain hours on certain days. It's just a different way of looking at time.'

The main difference between the work experiences of these two young women is trust. Laura works in a trusting culture, where she is expected to meet objectives without needing to be micro-managed. Essentially, she is treated as an adult. Her friend works in a low-trust environment where people are assumed to be inherently unreliable and prone to abuse 'the system' unless the boss keeps a close eye on their every move. She is managed as if she were a troublesome toddler.

It is not difficult to see which of these environments is more likely to encourage initiative, creativity and a willingness to put in extra effort, rather than simply counting down the hours to going-home time. Nor is it difficult to see which environment is more likely to attract and keep good employees.

Laura lists the benefits of having a trusting manager and working in a progressive department. 'There is flexibility that allows you to work in *your* most productive way,' she says. 'You may work better late at night or be working with business partners in another time zone. In my experience, more work gets done in a flexible workspace environment because I can take care of things like getting my car registered. I can work hours at home when I would normally be traveling to and from work. I can do focused work without the distractions that come with sitting at my cube, and I can be completely accessible for tasks that can be handled over email.'

In the first half of this book, we set out the consequences of freeing people to work in the way that suits them. We have shown compelling evidence that it delivers better results for business, individuals and the environment. Given this evidence, why are companies not adapting faster to the new world of work? Why do many of them cling to unproductive, morale-sapping habits, such as requiring people's presence at their desks in a fixed location for long and often unsociable hours, when technology enables many tasks to be done more efficiently at a place and time of their choice? What will it take to break these old habits?

Barriers to change

It is useful first to examine the obstacles that must be overcome if employers are to compete with their most fleet-footed rivals and keep pace with the accelerating opportunities afforded by new technology.

The first is this crucial matter of **trust**. Managers are the key to success in making the shift to future work. They can also be the biggest barrier. Some managers fall for their own PR, believing that they represent the clever elite whose role is to exercise power and keep the rest of the workforce under constant surveillance. This may be a façade, however, beneath which anxiety and insecurity lurk. Managers are more likely to give their team a free rein if they are confident of their own skills and value to the organization.

It may not be the individual manager who is to blame, but the **corporate culture**. A manager may want to give her people greater flexibility but feel crushed by dominant expectations that presence and long hours equal commitment. As one senior executive at a multinational technology company puts it: 'The view here is that we only hire "go-go" people. If people start talking about wanting balance and flexibility, they are no longer seen as "go-go" people.'

Such attitudes are often entrenched in organizations that are still wedded to **hierarchy**. Hierarchy thrives in many large organizations and the 'alpha' personalities who rise to the top are often driven by a desire for status based on their rank in the structure. For them, the trappings of power are alluring. There are still bloody battles for the corner office, even in some of today's supposedly flatter, 'matrix'-type companies. To managers naturally disposed to hierarchy, a radical change in the way people work poses a threat. Giving people the power to control their own work feels to some managers like a loss of face, as well as a loss of face time.

Then there is the barrier of **inertia**. What's the point of trying to change the system, the argument goes. Okay, people aren't exactly happy round here, but the company is still functioning fine, and besides, this is the way we've always worked. It's too hard to change.

Guy Laurence, head of **Vodafone**, the mobile technology operator, in the UK, spends a lot of time talking to senior executives from other companies about the benefits of future work. 'The biggest problem is getting companies to believe they can do it for *their* company,' he says. 'The chief executive wants to change but doesn't want to be the first in the sector. Organizations are scared of change and they think it's extremely complicated to move from the old style to the new style. They don't realize the technologies needed to support this are freely available in the marketplace.'

Laurence insists there is no business that technology-enabled future work cannot improve. 'Even if it's a production line, a third of the company will be non-production line, back-office, staff who could be using technology to work this way.'

There are many **myths**, too, that stand in the way of progress to future work. Flexible working arrangements, although a boon to many individual employees, have helped to perpetuate these myths. Governments have pressed employers to adopt flexible working practices as a way to 'help' employees in particular circumstances, working parents and caregivers being the main beneficiaries. As a result, flexible work programs are seen as a measure to accommodate certain employees' needs, rather than a strategy to drive business results.

'Employers think it's costly and disruptive,' says Caroline Waters, director of people and policy at **BT**, the UK communications group, and a pioneer of new working practices. 'They also think that employees won't work if they are given flexibility. Managers think they'll lose control – the fact is they never really had control just because they were co-located. There's often a failure to see it as anything other than home-based working – and many managers will write it off if they think it means people will be working from home all the time.'

Flawed attempts at introducing flexible working policies have made things worse, she says. 'Employers try to prescribe flexibility, which can't be done. Some say: "We've introduced a policy of people going home at 5 pm on Fridays". But that blanket approach doesn't work for everyone, and it doesn't represent true flexibility. The flexible working legislation in the UK stipulates that hours are agreed in perpetuity. This was put in to protect people from unscrupulous employers, but it puts many organizations off. Business changes every six months. Why put something in "forever" which in itself becomes a barrier to business flexibility?'[2]

Moving to the new world of work takes courage. As we showed in Chapters 5 and 6, some pioneering leaders have already taken the plunge. In some cases, they have had to 'unlearn' their default mode of wanting to control people and situations. They have also had to work hard at management skills such as communicating clearly and consistently.

Being a manager and a leader is not about standing still. If competition, globalization and new market opportunities require you to be adaptable and good at 'managing uncertainty', why should the same not apply to the vital task of managing people?

Five principles for progress

We have drawn up five principles for organizations that want to make a successful transition from the old to the new world of work. These are based on the business and socio-economic case for change, the large body of research on motivation and the effective approaches we have encountered in our research.

We call them the 'TRUST' principles (**Figure 8.1**).

Principles
1.　**T**rust your people
2.　**R**eward output
3.　**U**nderstand the business case
4.　**S**tart at the top
5.　**T**reat people as individuals

Figure 8.1 TRUST principles

You may wonder why technology does not figure in this list of principles. Clearly, people need the right infrastructure and equipment if they are to be able to work 'anytime anywhere'. Technology is an essential tool, or enabler, for the new world of work. Without any concomitant change in the *rules* of work, however, technology enslaves rather than liberates people.

'Anytime anywhere' easily becomes 'always on'. People are expected to be at their desks during regular working hours and then to be available on their Blackberry or cell phone outside these hours. As individuals, we must get better at pressing the 'off' switch. But we cannot do this if the culture of the organization continues to expect and reward people's physical (or virtual) presence round the clock.

Technology offers us a wonderful opportunity to 'free' time. First, it can end the tyranny of clocking up fixed hours in a fixed workplace by enabling work to be done regardless of time and place. This can then free up time for people to combine their work with the other things they want, or need, to do in their lives. This freedom, in turn, can motivate them to contribute their ideas and expertise freely, over and above their contracted hours, because they are treated as adults and trusted to get the job done.

It is not technology but the approach taken by management that enables this opportunity to be seized – or prevents it. Putting the technology in place is relatively easy. What is harder is to gain cultural acceptance of the need for a change in working practices. Managers may have to challenge and change their own assumptions about their role if they are to free people to be most effective in the new world of work.

1. Trust your people

Time and again in our discussions with business leaders and managers, trust emerges as the essential ingredient when people are liberated to do their best work. Trust is a two-way process, requiring open-mindedness and adaptability on both sides. In the first three chapters of this book, we investigated the high level of disillusionment and disengagement in today's workforce and the evidence that people are more likely to produce outstanding results if they are self-directed rather than micro-managed. We saw how money is only one of a range of motivations for work, and how fulfillment and engagement come from other aspects of work such as flexibility and choice over how it is done, recognition and new challenges.

Syd Nadim, founder and chief executive of **Clock**, an award-winning, UK-based digital marketing agency, says his job is 'to provide an environment for people to be brilliant'. Employees are equipped with laptops, broadband, instant messaging tools and videoconferencing so they can work where and when they want, apart from core hours of noon to 2 p.m. when they are expected to be in the office. 'If someone is doing an office day – not working from home or abroad – then they need to turn up at some point.'

Nadim offers this relative freedom as a tool to attract and retain talented designers and software engineers. Staff turnover is low and some employees have continued working for Clock after moving abroad, bringing in new business. In 13 years, only one person proved unreliable enough not to have his contract extended. Because people can choose when to work, the office is staffed for extended hours, with different employees working there between 7 a.m. and 10 p.m.

The office remains the center of activity, even though most employees can work from home when necessary. 'We have realized the downside in people missing out on the office banter and most importantly the collective knowledge pool,' says Nadim. 'Those who work abroad try to come into the office at least once a quarter so that they don't miss out on the important relationships that are developed within the company.'

Employers often take the view that only people who have proved their worth and reliability should be 'allowed' to decide how they work. Nadim, however, believes that trust is better engendered than earned.

'If you really trust people and really rely on them, they are more reliable and trustworthy,' he says. 'The approach has to be genuine otherwise people will see through it. If they know you don't really trust them and you've got a "plan B", it's easier for them to let you down. Let go and watch how well other people can deliver and perform.'[3]

2. Reward output, not input

To break free of the old model requires a radical change in the way work is rewarded. Future work will only fully succeed if the number of hours worked is decoupled from 'success'.

Under the prevailing model in many organizations, even salaried employees are expected to put in their minimum contracted hours – and to work considerably more to be seen as 'dedicated', 'loyal' and 'conscientious'. This is a deeply ingrained belief that can only be overturned through a well-orchestrated change program, driven from the top.

Ending the long-hours culture is a critical step on the path to future work. The argument for this change is very simple. People who work efficiently get the job done in a shorter time than those who are less efficient. People who take a long time to do their work are probably wasting time and are certainly not as productive per hour. People who are paid by results have every incentive to think up smarter ways of getting the work done. Their reward is more 'spare' time for them to use as leisure or to generate more income.

Managers have historically been bad at defining and measuring the output from work because the Industrial Age model judges and rewards people for their time. They have described work as a series of tasks – the job description – instead of approaching work in terms of results, goals or targets.

In future work it is results that count. Work is about the purpose, and the focus of management is on achieving that purpose. What is achieved is important; how the individual achieves it matters less.

At **Google**, people are judged on their results, not the time they put into their work, says Matt Brittin, head of the internet group's operations in the UK and Ireland. 'I can't remember having a conversation with anybody about their hours.'

Everyone has quarterly objectives, and their manager reviews their performance, scores them and measures them against their peer group. Performance feeds into pay and quarterly and annual bonuses. Objectives are set for the next quarter and coaching is given for areas that need improvement. 'Not many companies do quarterly reviews. It's a very good discipline for finding out capabilities that aren't up to scratch and addressing them.'[4]

Another company that has quarterly objectives and reviews is **Vodafone UK**. As a leader who believes in managing by output, Guy Laurence has the five 'big-ticket' objectives of each of his 100 top managers captured in a single electronic chart. Managers have to negotiate with each other to ensure that departments and resources are lined up to achieve the objectives, which are reviewed and revised every 12 weeks.

Laurence says managing by output means trusting people to manage themselves and use common sense. It does not mean the culture is soft or lacks discipline. 'We have a backbone but we don't live by the backbone,' he says. If anyone abuses the freedom, 'we'll have a quiet conversation with them, and if they continue to abuse it we let them go'. This does not happen often, and peer pressure usually takes care of any problems. 'If you move to team-based objectives and measure on output, it's mostly self-regulating. If one person lets the side down, someone else picks them up on it.'[5]

The US system known as Results-Only Work Environment, or ROWE, is centered on the idea of management by output. Initiated at Best Buy, the consumer electronics company, it has now been adopted by other organizations, including the Outlet division of **Gap**, the clothes retailer. At the end of this chapter, we feature a case study demonstrating the business benefits that Gap has obtained so far and where it hopes to go next.

3. Understand the business case

In every case where we have found organizations whole-heartedly embracing new working practices, the reason is a business one. It may be that the company is losing talented people (see Gap case study below). It may be that there are risks to business continuity, whether from severe weather, pandemics or terrorist attacks. It may be that the company has a technological advantage and wants to translate this into more efficient ways of working, as in the case of Microsoft in the Netherlands in Chapter 6. Or it may be a combination of factors.

Each organization has to establish its own business case for moving to future work. This can be a challenge. As with any big change, the case has to be made, often in the teeth of resistance. 'The pain is upfront in proving the case,' says Waters at BT. However, the many business benefits highlighted in Chapter 3 will help you understand the potential gains for your organization. The important thing to remember is that this is about doing better business, not just about being nice to people.

In his critically acclaimed book *Employees First, Customers Second*, Vineet Nayar explains how he turned management orthodoxy on its head at **HCL Technologies**, the Indian IT company, by making managers accountable to employees. We would agree with his argument that creating a culture of trust and a sense of common ownership is crucial to enable employees to give their best. 'Putting the customer first' should never be at the expense of the employee or it will backfire, since employee satisfaction is intimately linked to good customer service. We also believe the transition to future work should be underpinned by business goals. Offering alternative work patterns simply to suit individual employees is unlikely to bring about the fundamental changes in the work model that will benefit the business. Unless it is business-driven, any improvements in 'flexibility' will be subject to the whim of individual managers and may be short-lived.

Manufacturing is not an obvious place to encounter a 'give-and-take' relationship between management and staff. But Stuart Fell, owner of **Metal Assemblies**, a medium-sized engineering firm in the West Midlands, the traditional heart of England's manufacturing industry, believes in two-way flexibility based on trust. Employees at the company, which makes pressed metal components for car manufacturers such as Nissan and BMW, must be flexible in responding to sudden changes in customer demand, and managers must be flexible in responding to employees' 'real world' responsibilities.

Most of the work has to be done in shifts round the clock at the fixed location of the metal presses. Even so, within the 100-strong workforce there are about 50 different working arrangements, which fluctuate over time as their needs, and those of the business, change.

Fell describes it as a symbiotic relationship. 'The needs of the business can frequently be met better by people who also are having their needs met,' he says. 'I could name employees who would not work for us were it not for the flexibility we offer. I also know there is business we have won because we have been able to respond quickly to a customer demand . . . The organizations that don't adapt will end up the dinosaurs. They won't be able to move fast enough or recruit people to work for them.'[6]

4. Start at the top

As with any major change program, leadership needs to come from the top. To shift to a new work model, senior leaders must not only encourage their people to change, but also change themselves. Otherwise, attempts to adapt and thrive in the new world will remain confined to small pockets within an organization and risk being snuffed out by a dominant culture that is inclined to stick to 'the old ways'. A strategy that produces strong results for the business and for individuals should not have to rely on the lone efforts of a single pioneer manager or department.

The CEO may be an early champion of change who instinctively grasps the business case. The stimulus may come from outside, such as an imminent threat to business continuity, or an urgent need to cut costs while maintaining productivity. Or the chief executive may have to be persuaded by an influential colleague or a successful trial in a business unit. However it happens, the leadership team must be convinced, in order to convince others. The best way to do this is to demonstrate that the change applies to them too.

This is very different from the adoption of flexible work policies, which in large organizations are introduced and implemented by the HR department, and in small firms tend to be offered on an *ad hoc* basis. These policies are add-on programs rather than a whole new way of working.

Leaders and managers have to learn how to let go, rather than to control. 'Don't dictate, delegate' is a useful maxim. This will be harder in some national cultures than others. In Chapter 6, Theo Rinsema, general manager of Microsoft Netherlands, and Harry Brouwer, chairman of Unilever in Germany, Austria and Switzerland, explained how they changed their own attitudes and ways of working, and described the benefits that resulted.

Openness and adaptability should be attributes of today's leaders and should be integrated into leadership development. Unconscious biases (which we all have) can act as a barrier to the acceptance of different leadership styles and help to perpetuate a monoculture in the upper echelons of business. One of these biases is likely to be that 'presence equals commitment'. Many of today's leaders grew up in a 'face time' culture and can find it hard to see that this is not the only way to be effective. Surfacing and addressing these hidden biases is an increasingly important part of leadership development in progressive companies.

It is also part of the leader's role to demonstrate the importance of maintaining a healthy balance, and we address the need to manage technology-induced overwork later in this chapter and Chapter 9. Niall FitzGerald, former head of Unilever, has described how he altered his work habits after his younger daughter was born. He put a stop to breakfast meetings and kept weekends clear to spend more time with her. As he explained, his 'rather selfish choice' gave permission to his colleagues to change their own habits for the better. 'It's not about working less but about paying attention to the family,' he said.[7]

5. Treat people as individuals

To be successful in the new world of work, you have to treat people as the individuals they are. This is the essence of good people management and it is put to the test when people are working remotely or are part of a team dispersed across different regions or time zones.

Prescription and uniform solutions do not work. To produce their best, people need to be able to work in the way that suits them. Some are temperamentally suited to long spells of solitary work, making them ideal remote or home workers. But most people need regular contact with colleagues, and at least some of this must be face-to-face. Nor is everyone able or willing to work from home, even for some of the time. Home may be a place to escape from, rather than to.

Some people are highly self-driven, while others need deadlines, even artificial ones, imposed from outside to get down to the task in hand. Being in an office surrounded by other people working, or at least appearing to work, can be the motivation they need. People also work to different rhythms: there are early birds and night owls.

Managers, therefore, need to be highly adaptable. In the next section, we look at the skills that managers need to survive and thrive in the new world of work.

Unilever's principles for agile work

Under its 'agile working' program, launched at the end of 2009, Unilever is cutting office space with a view to making 30 percent of roles 'location-free' by 2015. The consumer goods multinational drew up the following principles, which were endorsed by senior business and HR leaders, for its new working practices:

- All employees may work anytime and anywhere as long as business needs are fully met
- Leaders must lead by example, working in an agile way themselves
- Performance is determined by results, not time and attendance – every employee has a personal work plan identifying desired results and how they will be measured
- Travel is to be avoided whenever possible
- Managers are assessed annually on how well they support agile workers and this feeds into the variable element of their pay

Unilever acknowledges that trade-offs include less personal space in offices and less face-to-face time with colleagues, and that the boundaries around personal time may be harder to manage. With proper implementation, however, it believes these trade-offs will be worthwhile. The company employs over 160,000 people in 100 countries. It says agility should help it reach its goal of doubling the size of the business without increasing its carbon footprint, and attract and retain talent, notably in Generation Y.

The policy is also explicitly linked with its goal of increasing diversity, especially women's representation in senior leadership. To achieve this, it is pushing hard to broaden the pipeline of female talent. It aims to raise the percentage of women managers from 40 percent at the start of 2011 to 55 percent by 2015. The target for women directors, the next level up from managers, is to go from 30 percent to 50 percent in the same time frame, according to Helen Wyatt, a senior human resources executive at Unilever.

The roll-out of agile working is one of the measures being taken to improve gender balance, along with more flexible careers, mentoring, networks and a focus on changing the organizational culture, says Wyatt, who previously worked at the global technology company HP.[8] Making more roles independent of location will help executives with caring responsibilities to manage the demands of relocating by enabling them to work partly from home, she adds. 'It will definitely help make international assignments more attractive. This type of working helps these roles to become less "extreme".'

All Unilever employees now fall into one of three work-style categories:

- Resident: working in the same facility most of the time
- Mobile: working in Unilever's or clients' facilities, at home, or while traveling
- Off-site: working mostly at a fixed location outside Unilever, such as a home office

Senior leaders are required to be role models by using agile working principles, technology and facilities themselves. Leading a dispersed international team also requires more disciplined and organized communication, says Wyatt. 'If people are all huddled together you can be more spontaneous.'

Culture is probably the biggest obstacle to making agile working happen quickly. 'Unilever has traditionally placed a huge premium on proximity and being face-to-face,' she says. 'It is still a big part of the psyche. Some of our leaders are embracing agile working, but others are not.'

What skills do managers need?

I do think there's a gap. Lots of managers don't understand that a critical aspect of the role they now have is to share what the business needs, to lay it out for people, and make sure they have the right skills and tools, and that people are then ever so sensible and bright about how to manage it themselves.

Caroline Waters, director of people and policy, BT[9]

Fortunately, managing in a future work environment does not mean learning a set of completely new skills. Some managers will adapt fairly quickly, because they simply need to extend the strong people skills they already possess. Others will need more help and support to develop the necessary skills. Even the most experienced senior leaders, however, admit they need to make some changes to their personal assumptions and management style, as we have shown in previous chapters.

The Future Work Forum at Henley Business School carried out research over ten years into the management of new working practices. It interviewed managers and HR directors and surveyed employees to establish what skills were required to run remote teams. It concluded that there was common agreement that managers have to work harder with such teams. Priorities may have to change, but they do not require radically different skills.

In a further study, it found that managers felt ill-equipped to deal with the day-to-day reality of managing remote teams. 'Almost half of respondents said that managers were unprepared for supervising flexible teams, and only a quarter had undergone specific training for managing remotely. In particular, anxiety around communication skills had been singled out and more support identified for developing better ways of binding teams together.'[10]

This finding is similar to that in the survey we conducted for this book, in which 60 percent of managers said they had never been trained to manage remote or flexible employees. At the same time, most of our respondents felt they had the right skills to do so.

What's needed is a fine balance between being more hands-off and more hands-on. This is not all about piling even more work onto the individual manager's already overloaded agenda. In many ways, it should be less onerous. Setting goals, and leaving it up to people how they achieve them, avoids the burdens of micro-management, such as checking time sheets and watching employees' every move. By freeing people to schedule their own work, individually or in teams, managers can save a lot of time and effort.

Instead, the focus is on the more interesting aspects of management – communicating, inspiring and motivating. These are leadership skills. In these areas, managers have to be more hands-on, in terms of organizing, planning and, crucially, communicating via many different media. They have to oversee the new rules of the game, such as ensuring that people know how to press the 'off' switch or dealing swiftly with any abuses of trust. This can be demanding, but extremely effective if done well.

We have grouped the skills needed alongside each of the five TRUST principles (**Figure 8.2**).

1. Trusting your people requires managers to be open to change, confident enough in their own competence and position to be able to delegate, enthusiastic about people's potential and willing to believe they will use their autonomy responsibly. Managers need to be good at building relationships, between themselves and their team and also between team members. They must be able to prioritize the things that really matter, because future work does not allow for micro-management. They should be constantly questioning and challenging of the 'way we do things', for example meetings for meetings' sake.

2. Rewarding output, rather than input, requires strong planning and organization. It needs an ability to negotiate, set and communicate clear objectives so that people know exactly what is expected of them. Managers should be good at inspiring and motivating people, even if they do not see them on a regular basis. They should be adaptable to the changing needs

Principles	Skills
1. Trust your people	■ Openness to change ■ Delegation ■ Relationship-building ■ Prioritizing ■ Challenging status quo
2. Reward output	■ Planning ahead ■ Clear objective-setting ■ Inspiring and motivating ■ Sensitivity to changing needs ■ Decisiveness and consistency
3. Understand the business case	■ Awareness of big trends ■ Stakeholder orientation ■ Technological competence ■ Influencing ■ Resilience
4. Start at the top	■ Willingness to change ■ Ability to 'let go' ■ Leadership by example ■ Time management ■ Tenacity
5. Treat people as individuals	■ Appreciation of difference ■ Responsiveness ■ Adaptability ■ Reliability ■ Team-building

Figure 8.2 TRUST principles and management skills

of the business, and able to communicate these quickly, and also sensitive to the changing needs of their team members. They must be decisive and consistent in tackling breaches of trust or poor performance to protect the benefits of future work and reassure everyone else that being responsible and accountable is valued.

3. Understanding the business case requires awareness of the big trends affecting business, work and society beyond the confines of the organization. Managers need to be alive to the changing expectations of internal and external stakeholders – employees, customers, suppliers, investors and regulators. They need to keep abreast of technological advances, though this does not necessitate becoming a geek. The important thing is to understand how technology can enable new ways of working, what is available, what investment will be required and what the payback will be. They need to be able to influence decision-makers and employees, and to be resilient in the face of resistance or inertia.

4. **Starting at the top** means leaders taking the initiative to move to future work. Since this will probably involve a change of culture, leaders need to be aware of their own style and what messages it sends to people. They have to be open to questioning their own assumptions about people and about established norms of work and careers. They need to be able to 'let go' and allow people to manage themselves, which may feel like taking a risk and stepping outside their comfort zone. They must represent the culture change visibly in their own behavior, whether that means dispensing with a private office, working from home once or twice a week or delegating more consistently. They will need to be highly efficient with their own time and work methods. In maintaining the new culture, they will require considerable tenacity.

5. **Treating people as individuals** demands sensitivity to differences between people, and an ability to turn these into strengths, both for the team and the wider business. This is particularly important when managing teams across different cultures, often working virtually, but applies to superficially homogenous teams working mainly from a single location too. Managers need to be quick in dealing with issues that arise, and prompt in responding to phone calls or messages from individuals working remotely. They have to be adaptable and good at building cohesive teams. Being a dependable communicator who makes time for each team member is essential.

Having set out the skills needed, we give detailed advice in Chapter 9 on how to apply these skills in practice. We explain what kind of rules you need in the new world of work, how to manage different individuals working remotely, how to build virtual teams and how to deal with managers' common concerns about the implications of the switch to future work.

We close this chapter with the story of how Gap, the global apparel brand, has begun to break free of the old model with a bold shift to results-only work in core parts of its North America business.

'Three-year competitive advantage' for Gap

High staff turnover prompted Gap, the clothing retailer, to begin a radical overhaul of working practices at its Outlet division in California in 2008. A year earlier, the division had started buying product from Asia via online auctions. The time zone difference meant that US production staff were often online working at 1 a.m., but were still expected to be at their desks in the office at 8 a.m.

These employees, most of them women in their 30s, tend to have long commutes to work because the high cost of real estate means many cannot afford to live near the office. Combined with the difficult hours, they were finding it impossible to balance their jobs with other personal commitments. 'Our staff turnover rate was 30–40 per cent and it was killing us,' says Eric Severson, senior vice-president of HR & communications for Gap North America and Outlet, in an interview in San Francisco.[11]

Traditional flexible work arrangements had failed to staunch the outflow. So Gap opted for an approach called (ROWE), first introduced at the Minneapolis headquarters of Best Buy, the consumer electronics company, by consultants Cali Ressler and Jody Thompson. This approach measures and rewards people for output, not hours, leaving it to individuals to decide where, when and how to carry out their work.

'It's like being back in college,' says Severson. 'People are held accountable for what they achieve rather than how much time they spend on a project or where they do the work. As in school, it doesn't matter how long or where you study – only if you pass the test. Ironically, employees love the freedom of ROWE so much that they are protective of the program, and put peer pressure on slackers to straighten up.'

Right from the first trial, the HR team measured the business impact to have a sound basis for pressing ahead or dropping the experiment. After six months, it recorded a halving in the attrition rate of staff in the production and technical design department, which supplies Gap's Outlet and Banana Republic Factory stores. The apparel sourcing organization in Asia, with whom they work, reported an increase in responsiveness and productivity in the US team.

Senior leadership at Gap wanted more proof before agreeing to roll it out across the division, says Severson. Another pilot, this time across functions from merchandising to store support, produced similar results. 'Employees, managers and internal customers all reported better service quality, timeliness and productivity, and staff turnover went down.'

After a third successful six-month pilot, the scheme went live across the division's head office in 2009. 'It has given us at least a three-year advantage over our competitors,' he says. 'Retail is very old school and we knew our competitors would be incredibly reticent to do this. But control over time is more precious to talent in this market than having more money, which they can get somewhere else.' In 2011, the scheme was expanded to employees at Gap North America headquarters, and other Gap divisions were actively considering implementing it.

Employers' resistance to giving people autonomy is often based on fear that they will desert their desks, abuse their freedom and be impossible to contact. Such fears proved unfounded at Gap Outlet, where there has been no wholesale desertion from the office. The main change, says Severson, is that people arrive and leave at different times, often before or after the rush hour, and that most of them now work at home once a week. Another objection raised was that people would be unavailable in the event of a 'fire drill', the term used for crises requiring all employees to be on site. This also proved to be an unwarranted fear. 'It's a principle of ROWE that there are no fire drills,' says Severson. 'This causes you to challenge your mentality. A fire drill isn't necessary most of the time. It's often the result of someone failing to plan ahead. We actually saw more responsiveness and flexibility to urgent business needs with ROWE, not less. The idea that being in the office makes one more responsive is a myth.'

The Outlet head office employs only a fraction of Gap Outlet's US workforce of about 14,000 employees. Introducing a version of ROWE in the stores, where 90 percent of employees work, would be much harder, but Severson does not rule it out. Indeed, he sees it as a way to encourage bright sales staff, who are typically college students, to make a career at Gap rather than going into other professions. 'This is where the heart of the business resides, and *that* would be the revolution. It's my next challenge.'

He believes that, with some imaginative thinking, store-based employees could have greater autonomy. For example:

- They could use Web-based technology to draw up schedules and organize shift swaps within teams, instead of managers administering schedules and having to approve changes. This would free store managers to focus on merchandising and other leadership tasks.
- District managers, who are responsible for a large number of stores, could save time traveling if store managers used technology such as an iPhone or iPad to take photos or give them a virtual tour of the store so they could see what was happening.
- Store managers could carry out some of their tasks, such as processing reports, at home.

'Employees are quite ingenious when they're asked to figure things out,' he says. 'We said we wouldn't invest in buying phones for our production and technical design teams, so they had to work out how to call Asia at night without long distance phones. They used instant messaging to ask their Asian colleagues, who were at work, to call them back.'

One issue with ROWE is that it does not necessarily reduce the number of hours people work, but just enables them to distribute those hours in a way that suits them better, he says. Gap has found that people work *more* hours, partly because many are now at home one day a week, making productive use of time they would otherwise spend commuting.

Giving people the freedom to work anywhere, anytime, is not always enough, he says. It needs to be combined with more effective work techniques to avoid the overload that many workers experience. These can be simple things like:

■ Turning off incoming emails to avoid distractions. Multitasking is less productive than working on one task after another, says Severson. 'I was responding to emails all day long. When I started dealing with them in bunches, three times a day, I became more productive. I find if I let them accumulate and prioritize what I have to do, other people solve the problems they could have solved on their own from the beginning.'

■ Time tricks. It helps to keep meetings to 45 minutes and minimize the use of slides. Start meetings at 15 minutes past the hour and finish on the hour.

Nevertheless, he describes ROWE as 'the perfect marriage of employee and business needs, with neither getting sold short'. He sums up the lessons from Gap's experience so far:

■ Change will not happen without the backing of the CEO and the leadership team.

■ Pilot, pilot and pilot again.

■ Managers need to brush up on their communication and planning skills.

■ Rules are important, for example making sure people put their cell phone numbers on the shared calendar so everyone can keep in touch.

CHAPTER 9

Putting it into practice

We spent a lot of time when designing and launching the strategy to be clear what it was and what it wasn't. It wasn't an HR program or benefit. It really was a business strategy. It wasn't just something mothers or working women used but something everyone uses every day.

Marcee Harris Schwartz, BDO USA[1]

We have shown the wide-ranging benefits of future work practices. The most successful examples grow from the values of the business founders or from strong leadership. For a manager lucky enough to work in such an environment, introducing a new work model will be relatively straightforward. For others it will be more of a challenge, pushing back against deeply ingrained habits. Based on our experience of working with, and talking to, hundreds of managers in organizations undergoing such change, this chapter sets out the practical steps to implement and sustain effective twenty-first century work.

First, it is good to know why you are doing it. Alternative work patterns, generally in the form of 'flexible working arrangements', are often introduced by HR departments as a policy which managers must follow, without a clear business case. They may be driven by legislation, employee requests, union pressure or 'diversity' goals, or they could be the result of a rationalization of space designed to save costs.

This is not enough. They need to be presented as a full-blown strategy to boost the bottom line. Only this way can future work produce the greatest benefits in terms of productivity, creativity and loyalty. It requires a change of culture from 'do what you are told' to 'do it the way that works best'. If implemented properly, it can make a huge difference to the lives of almost everyone in the enterprise. This chapter is about how to implement it, what works best and how to overcome resistance, using the TRUST framework introduced in Chapter 8.

The Way We Work program

Hertfordshire County Council, in the southeast of England, set about rationalizing its office portfolio in 2005, reducing it from 62 buildings to just four, saving revenue costs and releasing capital to invest elsewhere. But the council soon realized it needed a broader approach to gain the full benefits. 'What started out as a relocation program turned into a massive cultural change,' says David Robinson, program director of 'The Way We Work'.

The council asked employees what was preventing them from being more efficient and were told 'Give us IT that works.' It made a major investment in providing technology that allowed people to perform their jobs effectively, an investment that was easily covered by the large savings in occupancy costs.

The relocation program was used as a catalyst to introduce new ways of working. For some employees the extra traveling time was an incentive to try working from home, but for many it was an opportunity to review their personal work pattern and try something different. By the end of the five-year program, 47 percent of the staff had changed the time and/or place they worked.

The initiative had full support from senior management, with the program director reporting directly to the chief executive and the leader of the council. Directors and heads of service set an example by sitting in open-plan office space with their staff. Champions were appointed in each department to sell the ideas to managers and staff. But not all managers were keen to change.

According to Robinson, 'we had some old-fashioned managers who would only trust their people if they were in the office at 9 a.m. But the role of a manager in 2010 is very different from that in 2005. We've provided help, training, advice, guidance, but eventually for those that were unable to adapt we provided a speedy exit route.'

It took five years, with carefully planned steps along the way. The transformation has attracted huge interest. Robinson has hosted over 70 other local authorities. Many visitors have said they would love to introduce a similar scheme but their chief executive and senior officers would not support the changes.

Other councils have attempted smaller change programs with less success. They have tried rationalizing their office space, sharing services with other authorities or offering flexible working, without treating it as a major cultural change. 'The secret to it all is having one overall program,' says Robinson.[2]

1. Trusting your people in practice

The key to the successful implementation of future work is an understanding of when and how a job can be performed. One of the first steps is to analyze the constraints and see what tasks can be performed outside conventional hours and away from the normal workplace. If a job involves face-to-face contact with customers, it might have limited flexibility in terms of location but still allow a choice of hours for employees. In retail, for example, demand for extended hours of service creates a need for people to cover early and late shifts.

In many sectors, it's useful to start with the counter-intuitive assumption that the work can be done whenever an employee chooses and then restricts the scope based on logical constraints. It is also helpful to assume that work can be split up into units that do not have to be full-time jobs.

So, instead of designing jobs by listing a series of tasks, the future work manager begins with the outcomes and describes what needs to be achieved. This way she can come up with creative ways of getting work done and not just repeat old working patterns.

Managers often struggle with the idea that a job can be done outside the office, simply because it has never been tried. They assume that, because the whole job cannot be performed remotely, none of it can be. Yet most organizations that introduce future work practices end up with hybrid arrangements. Some work is performed in the office during normal working hours, some may be done at the same desk outside conventional hours and some may be done remotely, both inside and outside normal hours.

Where managers have fully implemented future work they may have as many different patterns of work as they have employees. While this sounds like a recipe for chaos, it manages itself well – provided the manager is prepared to trust people to get on with it.

What happens in practice is that people get together to work out how to achieve their business goals at the same time as meeting their personal requirements. If they do this as a team, with the support of their manager, they take ownership of the solution and make sure it works. If someone has to make a change to the new arrangement, he or she will first agree it with a colleague and then tell their manager. They present an answer, not a problem, since they have been handed the responsibility and have a vested interest in making things work. This contrasts with the convention of managers deciding a rota and being left with a problem if an individual falls sick or needs to make a change.

This is empowerment in action. It gives people more control over the time and place that they carry out their job, on the assumption that they will act responsibly and not abuse it. It is based on trust – and it works.

Sainsbury's, the UK food retail chain, has found that self-scheduling works best in small teams of 10–15 people. It has piloted this on food counters, such as bakery departments, and filling stations.

'We've said to them: Put together schedules you think will work and try them for a month,' says Rhona Caldwell, human resources manager for Sainsbury's in northwest England. 'In 99 per cent of cases it has worked, with a few tweaks. The teams manage issues better themselves. People work for people, not for organizations, which they see as a bit faceless. Small teams will spot if somebody is not very happy. When people get support, they want to come to work.'

In the new world, managers who feel the need to control their minions' every move will have difficulty. Those who see themselves as catalysts for people to perform at their best will adapt quickly.

Social media: enemy or friend of the corporation?

The way companies respond to the use of social media is a good reflection of their attitudes to trust. A 2010 survey of 1400 companies in the US found that 54 percent ban any employee use of sites such as Facebook and Twitter.[3] Others allow limited use, but only 10 percent provide complete freedom. The assumption is that people will spend hours tweeting to their friends or gossiping with colleagues. Worse still, they may spread malicious rumors about their managers or criticize the company. But what does this say about the attitude toward the people they hired to work for them? Obviously employees can't be trusted to use these tools sensibly, so banning them is the easiest option to avoid putting temptation in their way.

However, organizations that have embraced social media have found that they can create significant business advantage. Employees use information technology to improve communications with their colleagues and do not spend all their time socializing with their friends. If they are being judged by their output, they know that it is in their own interest not to get distracted. They also know that if they are trusted to use social media sensibly, they work for an organization that treats them like adults, and they live up to this.

BT is reaping the benefits of social media at work. 'Our policy is to be completely open,' says Caroline Waters, head of people and policy, 'We're very clear about what's appropriate and what isn't and about the consequences. We've had a handful of problems but those individuals would have been a problem anyway – it's not the technology. We have around 15,000 BT people on our own various Facebook sites and we have our own BT Wikipedia to help share and manage knowledge on a global basis. We are happy for people to use technology sensibly for their own use. We'd rather people were spending a few minutes doing something that was vital for them and getting it out of the way so that they are not distracted.'[4]

2. Rewarding output in practice

Once people are working 'out of sight', whether at home, on the road or in a virtual team scattered across different countries, managers are forced to focus on output. Instead of measuring the hours that someone puts into the job, they have to measure the results.

Goals have to be set that allow people to work without constant supervision. The manager and employee must have a clear understanding of what outcome is required. By expressing the goal in terms of a tangible product, both parties can be sure that they are aiming for the same result and there are no nasty surprises when the work is submitted. The goal should specify quality as well as quantity. There is no point in an employee beavering away for a month and producing the right number of outputs only to find that they are not of the quality expected.

It is critical that the work is not just expressed as a job description but as a series of targets that are understood and agreed by the employee. Once this has been established, it is much easier for the manager to let the individual get on with it because she no longer has to look for proof of effort. She has the results to show that the work has been done.

At first, deadlines for goals can be quite short term. Daily or weekly checks on output may be needed, but these can stretch to monthly or longer deadlines as confidence grows between manager and employee. This will be an individual arrangement. Two employees doing similar jobs might have different deadlines or report-back times based on their experience and competence.

At the start, some employees will welcome tight deadlines as a way to maintain their own concentration on the job. People used to working under supervision can find themselves distracted when working at home or varying their working time. Some people need to learn new ways of managing themselves.

We have shown how workers who are given autonomy generally report big improvements in productivity. Good managers see the benefits of this and stop rewarding long hours and insisting on people being present when it's not strictly necessary. Instead of having to put in additional hours in the workplace to demonstrate 'dedication' to the job and the company, the objective is to complete a quality job in the shortest time.

3. Understanding the business case in practice

Organizations need a clear plan for the transition to future work, outlining the business objectives as well as the stages of implementation. Managers will embrace the move to future work more willingly if they understand that it has clear business goals. If they see it as another piece of bureaucracy to stop them getting on with their jobs, they will greet it at best with apathetic acceptance and at worst with downright antagonism.

This is as important as introducing a brand new product line, taking over another company, launching additional services, relocating the business or selling off a division. It is a major step in the development of the business and should be treated as such.

It should be discussed, understood and agreed by the board. This is not easy. Board meetings often consist of facts, figures and tangible data. Here we are talking about the way we work, the atmosphere in the organization, the relationship we have with our people and what we are doing to their lives. It is about HOW we manage, not just WHAT we manage. Because some of this can be seen as soft and intangible, it is vital to have as many data to hand on the business benefits as possible (see Chapter 4 for the full panoply of benefits). Otherwise the issue risks being ignored and the culture remaining stubbornly unchanged.

Collect clear, measurable results from other companies and, preferably, from inside your own business, and link them to broader business goals. **BT** used peer group pressure to bring about change. 'Find people who really make it work,' says Caroline Waters. 'We found people's opposite numbers who were doing it and had all the right performance metrics. We held them up, gave them a platform, and brought them together in groups and at conferences. It changes the role of HR: the line managers do it, and you [HR] help them. One converted line manager is worth ten suits from HR. They're much more influential with their peer group than we could ever be.'[5]

Identify and cost the resources involved in making the change and clearly lay out timescales. Include the cost of additional information technology and any up-front investment. Offset this against the cost savings in real estate and the expected benefits from increased productivity. Translate this into increased output from existing staff, or a reduction in headcount while maintaining current levels of output.

For most organizations, the transition represents a major change program and it needs to be planned and executed as such. Resources need to be allocated to the program and money set aside for management development. A realistic investment of leadership time is essential. A project team should be set up with representatives from operational management as well as specialists such as HR, IT and Real Estate. A senior project manager should be appointed with access to the leadership team and the authority to push the program forward when it comes up against the inevitable resistance from entrenched individuals.

Measure the impact of the changes from the start. Don't just measure employee engagement or satisfaction scores. Look too at productivity, customer service, cost savings on business travel and real estate, speed of entry to new markets, staff turnover, knowledge retention and the health of the workforce.

4. Starting at the top in practice

Selling the concept of future work has to top the list from the start. This is much more than a change in operational practices or the addition of a few more policies and procedures. It is a change of culture.

It will not happen if senior managers set themselves apart. In many organizations that offer flexible working policies, the implicit message from top management is: 'Yes, we allow our employees to work flexibly but managers need to be working full-on all the time.' Work–life balance is for the troops, not for the officers. In the most macho work environments, people brag about the long hours they work, just as heavy drinkers boast about how much alcohol they downed on a Friday night.

To be effective, a future work strategy needs visible support and momentum from a senior champion, or champions, preferably at board level. Getting top management backing is essential and the program manager will need to be politically astute to win over the skeptics.

Ideally the chief executive should be heading the initiative, not just paying lip service but demonstrating behavior that can be mirrored by managers throughout the company. The worst examples of so-called flexible workspaces have junior employees crammed together in poorly run hot-desking areas while senior managers maintain separate fiefdoms, luxuriating in their thick-carpeted personal offices. The best examples have the CEO and directors sitting in open-plan areas, symbolizing the abolition of traditional hierarchies.

'The first and most important step is leadership support and accountability,' says Marcee Harris Schwartz of **BDO USA**, the accounting firm. 'We spent a lot of time at the very beginning of the strategy design with the very top-level leaders at the firm, having them take real ownership of what the strategy was and how it was communicated ... A key differentiator for us is that our CEO, Jack Weisbaum, feels ownership of the strategy and speaks eloquently about the benefits. He works from his home office in Florida and travels quite a bit. He uses day-to-day flexibility. He speaks about how he will try and wrap up part of the day, go for a swim, have dinner with his wife, then log back on in the evening to interact with our West Coast leaders.'[6]

At **BT**, Caroline Waters says: 'We had to persuade Peter Bonfield [then chief executive], but when he got it, he got it. We had him talk about it.

We had a flexible working champion who was the chief executive of the retail business. It's exactly as we built our diversity agenda – bottom up and top down. Productivity went up and there were cost savings and reduced turnover, and managers knew their success was measured on these things, so rolling this out became another business tool.'

Future work practices must not rely on the enlightened leadership of a single manager, or they risk being reversed when that manager moves on or when the company merges with another organization that is culturally very different. These practices need to be part of the way the whole organization works. This is why they require the commitment of the entire leadership team, and a thorough understanding of the business case by middle managers, so there is no going back.

A US business had made big strides in enabling people to work from home some or all of the time, reducing office space and equipping workers with mobile technology. One team worked with colleagues around the world, and their hours extended well beyond the local business day, so this gave them much needed flexibility in the daytime. This manageable new model was broken by the arrival of a boss who decreed that everyone should be at an office desk during the business day. As a former employee explained, their jobs did not change, so this meant they were effectively forced to work day and night. It was a recipe for burnout, plummeting productivity and rock-bottom morale. 'The goal was for us to play as a team, but our team was not local, so sitting in an empty office had no rationale.'

Introducing future work is an opportunity to revisit the values of the organization and see how working practices align with them. Do the values reflect a respect for people and a belief that they will respond responsibly to being trusted? The implementation plan should be explicit about the values that lie behind the new practices. Employees can then test managers' behavior against the espoused values and point out where they do not live up to their public statements. This puts meat on the bones of statements such as 'our people are our most important asset' and 'we believe in equality and fairness'.

A useful tool for breaking down barriers to future work is 'reverse' mentoring of senior executives by Gen Y employees. The idea is that the young employees explain the uses and benefits of the latest technology and social media to top managers. Having this responsibility, and the ear of senior executives, is motivating for the junior employees, while their seniors gain useful insights into how the next generation thinks and communicates. An alternative version of this is reciprocal mentoring, where senior executives in turn give career advice to younger staff.

5. Treating people as individuals in practice

Traditionally, good managers have motivated employees by being seen, walking about and saying 'well done'. They have spent time getting to know people and have been available for a chat when needed.

As work becomes increasingly dispersed and virtual, they can no longer literally stand over people to see what is happening. Not all employees are self-starters. Some may need more encouragement and handholding during the early days of the new work patterns. If they are used to being given directions, they may take a while to feel comfortable about making decisions for themselves and getting out of old habits. It is important for managers to understand what motivates each individual and to adapt accordingly.

Treating people as individuals is an important aspect of future work. Because everyone is different, and employers need to get the best out of each person, working arrangements will vary. Managers often raise concerns about the potential for unfair treatment of employees if they do not all have the same work pattern. After many years of being told not to discriminate, they fear 'breaking the rules'. But this is to confuse fairness with equality. Future work is about treating people fairly without needing identical work arrangements for everyone. This presents a challenge to managers who prefer simply to follow a set of rules, as it requires them to use some judgment and actually manage.

In its management training, **Sainsbury's** has recently put the emphasis on individual judgment, says Rhona Caldwell. 'People in our organization can become too rule-bound,' she says. 'It's important to listen to colleagues and to treat them as individuals. The rules are just a framework. None of it is rigid. We say to them: What would you do if it were a member of your family?'

As with any big change program, employees need to know well in advance what is happening and how it will impact them. Managers should sit down with individuals and teams and discuss plans and options.

Where people have to be in face-to-face contact with customers, there is less scope for autonomous working, but where they mostly use telephones there is greater scope for change. Many jobs have an element of report writing, form filling or answering emails that can be done anywhere and anytime, provided the technology is available. These tasks are often performed more quickly and efficiently in the quiet of a remote location than in the middle of a noisy office. It may suit one individual to work from home one day a week to perform these 'solo' tasks and spend the rest of the time in the office interacting with colleagues. However, another person doing the same job may find home totally unsuitable for quiet concentration.

Addressing managers' concerns

Not surprisingly, many leaders and managers used to the conventional work model initially have misgivings about making the transition to the new world of work. In this section, we address the questions and concerns that commonly arise.

Q. How will I know they are working?

This is the biggest worry for managers faced with the prospect of people working remotely. They are concerned that individuals will spend all day watching television, talking to the neighbors or shopping or otherwise 'wasting time'.

'Will I have to phone them every morning to check they are out of bed and getting on with the job?' 'Do I need software that tracks their activities on their computer?' The answer is straightforward. If your people get the work done, then you will know that they have been doing the job. Moreover, if it is the kind of work that does not have to be done between fixed hours, checking when they are working is irrelevant. The only real test here is the quality, quantity and timeliness of the work output.

HSBC India has run workshops for managers and employees to prepare them for a more flexible work culture. Managers expressed concern that they would lose control, that productivity might fall and that it would not be possible to have the entire team present for 8 30 a.m. meetings in the office, says Nikunj Upadhyay, vice-president for organizational development. 'We talked about these issues and about getting used to alternative methods like meetings by phone. For example, the manager could be based in Mumbai but their team could be in Delhi. We asked them: "Why is it so important to see the person?" "Why does it matter as long as they are responding to you?" "Would *you* not have worked if you were working from home?" Managers can be so absorbed in being supervisors that they take a very rigid view of how, where and when employees should work. It requires dialogue.'[7]

Ask yourself how you can be sure that employees are working when they are in the office? Just because they are at their workstations, or tapping away at their keyboards, there is no guarantee that they are producing worthwhile results.

Q. Won't this open the floodgates?

Why would it matter if it did? Ideally, your strategy will be to create a wholesale shift in work styles, enabling everyone to have a greater degree of autonomy over where and when they work, as this will benefit the business and themselves.

Where the job or sector allows only limited choice over time or location, however, you should share around what flexibility is available. Think in terms of desired outcomes, not tasks (see under **Trusting your people** earlier in this chapter). Explain the business objectives to the team and ask them to come up with more efficient ways of achieving them.

There is no need to limit the variations in work patterns, provided business objectives are met. All individuals are different, so it is unlikely that any two work patterns will be identical. Some people like to start work early, while others are late risers. Some want to work longer days but shorter weeks, while others will prefer to take some work home to complete in the evenings. Provided customer needs are met, these variations do not need to be supervised. Experiment and see what works.

We recommend pilots and trial periods before making more permanent changes. Managers often fear that once they have agreed to something they cannot look back. But until it is tried out, neither party will really know if it is working. Once the benefits, such as greater productivity, extended customer service coverage or real estate savings, become evident, everyone will be more comfortable about taking the plunge.

If things do not work out at first, make adjustments and try again. Keep an open mind. Investigate whether the problem is really to do with the new working practices or is actually a specific performance issue, which needs to be dealt with separately.

Q. What happens to relationships and team spirit?

A common concern about new work styles is that team spirit will suffer. In a conventional workplace, people sit together and exchange ideas. They have coffee and lunch breaks together. They spend the first 20 minutes of the day chatting about traffic problems or last night's soccer match or soap opera. By virtue of sitting together, a team spirit is born. A good manager will nurture this and encourage people to collaborate.

In the new world of work, this teambuilding is at risk. How will people get a chance to build the informal relationships that tie the team together? Managers need to recognize the importance of informal communications between team members. If all contacts are about work, people will take a long time to get to know their colleagues. The few minutes each day sharing personal experiences that are unrelated to work are critical to maintaining team relationships.

For people who now see their colleagues once a week instead of once a day, this is no great problem. But there is an increasing chance that remote working, shifted hours and virtual teamwork across time zones mean that some people rarely see the rest of the team. Managers discover that there is hardly ever a time when all their people are together, whether virtually or in a physical office.

This is when it makes sense to build back some of the lost 'team time'. Team meetings can be arranged, perhaps monthly, to communicate the latest business information and get people to discuss their ideas. But it is equally important to compensate for the loss of casual chats about non-work topics. Arranging for people to take a coffee break during the meeting and encouraging everyone to go to the staff restaurant together for lunch is probably sufficient. However, more formal teambuilding exercises have their place and can reap real rewards in terms of improved collaboration, especially if people are dispersed across different countries and only meet rarely.

Managing people who work flexibly or remotely means 'you just have to do more of what you should be doing anyway', says Alison Gregory, a senior managing consultant for organization and people in **IBM** Global Business Services. 'You have to be more focused on outcomes, better at communication, more explicit about your expectations, more regular about checking that work is going the right way. You might have to schedule short, but more frequent, calls to chat with somebody working for you in another place. Team communication won't happen by accident when you walk by someone's desk, so you have to create that time deliberately.'[8]

Q. Don't we still need our meetings?

While face-to-face meetings are important for individuals and teams who spend most of their time working remotely, the conventional office meeting culture needs to be challenged. For a start, if more people are working anywhere anytime, a whole-day meeting will be difficult to arrange.

This is a great stimulus to question the purpose and value of routine meetings. Does the weekly update meeting on a Monday morning really need to happen at all? Can the information be communicated by email, voicemail or as part of a discussion forum on the intranet? If it requires feedback from participants, can this be given in a text form rather than verbally in a meeting room? What is the purpose of the meeting anyway? Is it just for sharing information or is it for making decisions? Can it be held by audio or video link so it is still live but people do not have to be in the same place?

In many conventional cultures, having a diary full of meetings and being seen as overloaded, to the point of being stressed, is a sign of importance. Not so in the world of future work. People are judged by their output, not the number of meetings they attend. In implementing a Results-Only Work Environment (ROWE), **Best Buy** set an informal rule that all meetings were optional. If people cannot see any use in the meeting, they do not go. This focuses the mind of the meeting owner on what he is trying to achieve and how he can make it compelling to the people he wants there.

There are many technologies available to achieve the desired results without taking up people's time and energy getting to a meeting room, from simple text solutions such as Instant Messaging to sophisticated Virtual Presence conferencing systems. It can take terrible events like the 9/11 attacks or the swine flu epidemic to make people stop and think about alternatives to the overflowing schedule of back-to-back meetings. We hope the benefits of future work will be realized without such disasters and tragedies in future.

This is not to say that all face-to-face meetings should be abolished. There are times when getting people in the same room to hear and discuss issues is the most effective way of achieving an objective. It is essential for relationship-building and consideration of sensitive and personal issues, such as leadership development. But the cost savings, and the environmental and human benefits, of reducing travel to physical meetings are powerful reasons to use alternatives such as videoconferencing wherever possible.

The global HR team at **Unilever** holds half of its seven to eight meetings a year via a Telepresence service provided by Teliris. 'It's a great discipline,' says Helen Wyatt of Unilever. 'We meet for less time and focus on priority items. If people fly a long way, they tend to make sure the meeting lasts two to three days to justify the journey.'

Better decisions using videoconferences

As a private equity firm with a global reach, Permira has offices in major financial centers around the world. It needs its project teams of experts from different offices to collaborate closely regardless of geography.

When it moved into new offices in London's Pall Mall in 2009, it doubled the number of videoconferencing suites to four to keep up with demand. Although only 90 people work in the building, the video meeting facilities are in constant use by staff at all levels.

'When we started with videoconferencing, people could see an immediate payback in saving time and money by reducing travel,' says Carolyn Lees, head of information technology. 'Now it is ingrained in the culture because it makes meetings work better anyway. Everyone uses it from the top down for all sorts of meetings, and there is no need for a champion to be promoting it.'[9]

To make sure the video connections work correctly, a technician puts in a test call to a new location and is on call during the meeting in case of problems. Despite the cost of providing and maintaining the equipment, the firm has seen major savings in the time and expense of international travel. There are no guidelines to tell people what type of meeting to hold over the system, and it is left to individuals to decide. 'They can see the improvement in communications at the touch of a button,' says Lees. 'You are in a much better position to be able to discuss, agree, make decisions, whatever it is you want to do. It is surely a contributor to better communications and therefore better decision making.'

Q. What happens to employment contracts?

Future work questions the need for a contractual employment relationship in the traditional sense. If it is possible to get the work done through a results-based arrangement, then employing someone by the hour or month makes no sense. It could simply be a service, purchased from a supplier as with any subcontracted relationship. An individual engaged under this relationship could be self-employed or might have an employment contract with an agency.

If an individual is working for an organization on a long-term basis, they will expect to have a more permanent arrangement than just a contract for their next piece of work. Employment legislation in most countries will insist that they have certain rights such as a minimum period of notice and paid vacation time. So employees will still have contracts setting out their rights and responsibilities but these are becoming more flexible as work patterns change. They may still have to specify a time and place of work but can often be varied by mutual agreement between employee and employer.

In some instances, labor laws have not caught up with the latest working practices and might still prevent an arrangement that suits the employer and employee. For example, in California a provision of the Labor Code prohibits employees working discontinuously in a 24-hour period. This was designed at a time when most work was shift work in factories. Now, unintentionally, this outdated labor law discourages employers from implementing results-based work for hourly employees because of the risk that they would face a prohibitively expensive class action lawsuit.

It is beyond the scope of this book to look into the details of contractual legislation everywhere, but it is clear from the numerous examples of future work across the world that major employers are devising working solutions that are legal. Since the flexibility of the labor market is a key factor in economic success, it is likely that legislators will be motivated to remove any serious roadblocks to prevent work from moving offshore to more flexible jurisdictions.

Q. What's in it for me?

The benefits of future work may be obvious to the project champion and the senior team leading the change, but the individual manager can see it as an unwelcome disruption. To overcome this, many organizations run management workshops to explain the benefits and reduce the fears. These provide practical information on how to manage flexible, remote and virtual teams and they give participants the confidence to experiment.

The idea of loosening control and empowering employees can be very threatening to a manager, particularly one who is insecure in his position. Future work can be seen as undermining his authority and hindering his ability to get the job done. It is important, therefore, that managers can see past the initial barriers and appreciate the benefits that will follow on.

Workshops can introduce the experiences of other organizations that have already gone through the change process and can be used to share experiences across the enterprise. If one department or business unit has successfully implemented new working practices, this story can be used to help others follow suit. Assembling a core of convinced managers will help to spread the word. Using them in the workshop and elsewhere will contribute to wider success.

Future work involves genuine autonomy for employees. This probably means the need for fewer middle managers. If employees are managing themselves and are trusted to work without close supervision, management resources are freed up. It should be possible for more people to be reporting to any one manager without any detrimental effects.

The manager's role also changes. Instead of being a taskmaster or micro-manager, she needs to be a skilled leader of people, a coach and a guide. The job is, therefore, both more exciting and more challenging. For those managers who want to retain control over people, the transition will be difficult or impossible. For those who can see the benefits of change and who relish the chance to motivate individuals and teams to produce the best results by treating them as adults, the future looks good.

Managing global, cross-cultural teams

Seventy percent of employees at IBM, the IT, software and consulting services giant, work at home at least once a week. Three-quarters of managers have people in their teams who work remotely, and whom they do not see on a daily basis. About 40 percent of the company's 400,000 employees are classified as mobile, with no fixed work base. Employees, other than those working in client contact or delivery centers, where uninterrupted service is necessary, have flexibility about where and when they work.

Gary Kildare, a global vice-president for human resources at IBM, stresses the importance of people skills in managing mobile employees and teams dispersed across the world, who collaborate virtually rather than face-to-face. 'You can be wonderful technically, but you also have to focus on people or it will hold you back as a leader,' he says.

Two things are really important: relationships and sensitivity. 'It can take longer to build trusting relationships because you don't always have that face-face contact with people. Leaders and managers must take time to understand how individuals are performing if they don't get to observe them directly every day in an office setting. It's about setting very clear goals and objectives and expectations and measuring the outcome.'

Communication is at the heart of it. 'I tend to use a lot of conference calls with my own team. This means setting a schedule one quarter (three months) in advance so people know when things are going to happen. I try to avoid missing or canceling calls unless it's inevitable. People like to see patterns and feel included.'

As for sensitivity, this is especially important in relation to cultural differences. 'There can be misunderstandings. When people send emails, there can be multiple or different interpretations. As a leader you mustn't make assumptions about anyone or anything. You can't speak 20 languages but you can respect everyone's culture. In some cultures, people are quiet, in others they are not. Some are very outspoken, some are less so. It's about treating and respecting everyone as an individual.

'You have to set standards and insist on team collaboration and involvement. You have to be quite tough if you feel someone has overstepped the boundary. We have a very intellectual, highly skilled workforce. Our people are graduates, double-degree holders, doctorates and extremely able. When we use email and instant messaging, people use different styles and sometimes they can be quite direct. It's important to think about what we write, just as much as what we say – adding a smiley face doesn't make a tough message any easier.'

Given the profile of the workforce, it is far more likely to contain committed 24/7 workers than people who are work-shy. How can managers act to stop people feeling that they have to be 'always available', given that the technology makes that possible?

'Managers will help if they see people who are online too much,' Kildare says. 'Managers are expected to help balance workload across teams and, if someone is struggling to meet a deadline, to make sure they're getting help and assistance needed. In team-oriented work environments, it's important for people to be staying in touch with colleagues. Often it's colleagues who tell you that you're doing a little too much.'[10]

In summary: principles, skills and practices

In **Figure 9.1**, we summarize the key principles and management skills again, together with the practices set out in this chapter to help you manage successfully in the new world of work.

Principles	Skills	Practices
1. Trust your people	■ Openness to change ■ Delegation ■ Relationship-building ■ Prioritizing	■ Start from the assumption that all jobs have some potential for future work ■ Discuss job with the employee and agree constraints to flexibility

Figure 9.1 TRUST principles, management skills and practices

Principles	Skills	Practices
	■ Challenging status quo	■ Give people as much freedom as possible to work the way that suits them best
		■ Don't insist that people work at specific times unless the job demands it
		■ Allow people to use social media appropriately
		■ Encourage people to work in teams even if they are not sitting together
		■ Challenge the need for meetings
		■ Don't keep work to yourself if it can be done by other people
2. Reward output	■ Planning ahead ■ Clear objective-setting ■ Inspiring and motivating ■ Sensitivity to changing needs ■ Decisiveness and consistency	■ Set clear outcomes and measure results ■ Hold regular reviews, particularly at first ■ Give plenty of feedback, with a personal touch ■ Don't micro-manage, but do check people aren't working 24/7 ■ Act quickly on poor performance or abuse of trust ■ Give people challenging work to develop them
3. Understand the business case	■ Awareness of big trends ■ Stakeholder orientation ■ Technological competence ■ Influencing ■ Resilience	■ Keep in touch with demographic, social and environmental trends, as well as business trends ■ Identify potential for reduced costs and increased productivity ■ Invest in technology to increase output ■ Monitor and measure the impact on business outcomes ■ Build results into business plans ■ Share successes across the business

Figure 9.1 (Continued)

Principles	Skills	Practices
4. Start at the top	■ Willingness to change ■ Ability to 'let go' ■ Leadership by example ■ Time management ■ Tenacity	■ Get senior management to support this as a major business and culture change program ■ Set an example by doing it yourself ■ Communicate the message that this applies at all levels ■ Use technology effectively to control your own workload ■ See it through as you would any change program that benefits the business
5. Treat people as individuals	■ Appreciation of difference ■ Responsiveness ■ Adaptability ■ Reliability ■ Team-building	■ Understand what motivates individual employees ■ Don't try and fit people into a fixed work pattern ■ Keep in touch with remote workers when you say you will ■ Use judgment and don't just follow rules ■ Help people to integrate work into the rest of their lives ■ Hold face-to-face meetings for dispersed and virtual teams

Figure 9.1 (Continued)

Following the guidance in this chapter will help you to move into the exciting world of future work. If you are a manager, you now have plenty of examples to follow. The challenge is to make it happen in your organization. In the final chapter, Chapter 10, we will look at where all the trends covered in this book are leading and give you a glimpse into the future that you have a chance to shape.

CHAPTER 10

Looking over the horizon

When Larry Smith joined IBM in the UK in the late 1980s, he used to make sure he walked past his manager's office after 6.30pm so his presence was noted. It was almost an unwritten rule.

Nearly 25 years later, he is still working for the company, but in a radically different way. He is a contractor, supplying his services via Persistent, one of IBM's preferred suppliers in India. He has done this for over a year without ever coming face-to-face with the people who manage him.

'I have never met my manager or any of his management chain, yet I lead his business development efforts which represent several million dollars of business,' he says. Asked where his boss is based, he has to check. It turns out to be Connecticut – though it could have been anywhere in the same time zone.

Larry's experience will seem alien, though possibly quite appealing, to legions of office workers around the world. He is an example of how the future of work has already arrived for individuals and organizations at the leading edge. He works closely with teams in India and China, talking to them weekly by phone and chatting online by IBM's in-house messenger every day, but he has never met any of them. Most of his colleagues are based in the US and China, while he works from home in Britain.

He also has a contracting role as part of an IBM global team developing cloud computing products. Again, he chats to this team on a daily basis but has not encountered any of them in the flesh, apart from the manager, whom he finally met after six months in the job.

'You have to be very self-motivated to work this way,' he says. 'I'm a self-starter and I'm good at planning my day. I have to be structured and organized. I don't work at weekends and normally not after 7pm on Fridays. But during the week my life and work are intertwined.'

If you work like this, you also have to be firm about drawing boundaries, or the job will take over your life. 'For example, on Wednesday night at 11pm I presented to 20 people in Sydney. At 9pm that night I was having a conference call with people in Austin, Texas, on a business proposal, which I presented at 7.30 this morning to people in Finland. On Tuesday night they wanted me to join some important conference calls but I was going down to the pub with my son to watch Tottenham [football club] play, so I refused to attend. I said: "Sorry, but I have a life. My family are important to me." '

As someone who works online, it was natural for Larry to use the Internet in his social life as well. He met his current wife, Sharon Boyse-Smith, a senior executive with Sony Music, through an online dating service. 'She's in a totally different industry and we would never have met without profiling on the internet.'

He says he has a far better quality of life in this virtual environment than spending time traveling to meet people. His manager completely trusts him to get the job done. 'He doesn't start work until many hours after me so he can't monitor what I am doing. If I want to take the dog for a long walk this afternoon, I just will.'

Larry believes all organizations will have to have this kind of relationship with their people in the future. 'Empowering professionals who are task-driven has to be the way forward. It's been pioneered in the IT industry but eventually everyone will offer it.'

How soon will this be? In our survey for this book, two-thirds of managers agreed there would be a revolution in working practices in the next decade.

Cloud cover

Forecasting is a hazardous business, especially as the technology that opens the way to these far-reaching changes is advancing so rapidly. IDC, the global market intelligence provider, describes the rate of internet innovation as 'breakneck'. In 2013, it says, the number of internet users worldwide will reach more than 2bn, or nearly one-third of the world's population.[1]

One thing that can be certain, however, is that technology will have an increasing influence on all our lives, particularly our working lives. Already it is difficult to remember what we did before the Internet existed. How did we cope before Google pointed us to the answers? In ten years' time we will look back on today's tools and think of them as clunky or quaint. We will also take for granted that connectivity is available wherever we are at speeds unimaginable today.

One development that will influence our work over the next few years is the growth of cloud computing. Instead of having ever more powerful desktop or laptop machines, the computing power is provided over the Internet and is available on demand like any other utility. While it's not a new idea, the latest portable communication devices combined with ubiquitous, secure networks make its implementation a practical reality. Large organizations can hold their data and applications centrally but accessible from anywhere. This allows them to free up employees to access information however they wish. For smaller businesses, a whole new raft of internet-based services is emerging to replace their aging technology.

WiFi hotspots are popping up all over the place and we will soon have 4G mobile services so everyone can work on the move. In the same way that individuals in the past chose their favorite pen and paper to take notes, they will decide their preferred way of accessing the cloud, whether it's an Apple iPad, an Android smartphone or a Windows netbook. Employers will no longer be responsible for issuing and maintaining a fleet of corporate laptops for employees to lug around.

Cloud computing will provide people with their office in their hand, enabling them to work where and when they want. 'Cloud removes location from the equation,' says Guy Laurence, Vodafone UK CEO.[2] 'You don't have to go to the office or be at home. It's wherever there's connectivity. People work best where there isn't a location requirement.' As an example of location-independent working, he points to 7causes, a Dutch marketing consultancy run and staffed by women that has its office in a converted bus. The consultants take the office to the client, working on the way, and avoid wasted travel time.

Cloud computing is already here in the form of Web-based services like Google Apps and its growing influence is just one of many developments on the horizon. What impact will these advances, and continuing globalization, have on work? There are enough trends already under way to be able to predict the likely shape of things to come. These are the main ones to watch:

From employment to deployment

Work will become more of a tradable commodity, rather than a job. There will be more independent contractors and freelancers. In the US, the percentage of work done by contingent workers has grown from 6 percent to more than 27 percent in the past 20 years, according to the Human Capital Institute, a US-based global association for strategic talent management.[3]

Contractors and consultants will bid for work online and will be paid for results. This is an emerging form of what has been termed 'crowdsourcing' – using the power of the Internet to allocate tasks to people anywhere in the world by issuing a request for work. In the last few years, this has been largely associated with finding volunteers to contribute their expertise for free. The whole free, open-source software movement is based on this model and there are high-profile examples such as Wikipedia, the free encyclopedia. However, there is now a growing market for paid work via the Internet.

Since 2005, Amazon has run its Mechanical Turk as a marketplace for work that allows requesters to pose 'Human Intelligence Tasks' and pay people to perform them. These are typically simple repetitive tasks, such as searching for information on the Web, paid a few cents for each successful result. At the other end of the scale is Innocentive where cash awards of up to a million dollars are given for successful solutions to research problems.

These markets cut across established employment patterns. Workers are paid for results but have no employment rights or benefits. There is no question of paying a minimum wage, expressed as a rate per hour, since this is results-based work and time is irrelevant. It's a very attractive model for businesses able to allocate work across the Internet as they can choose suppliers who will perform tasks for a fraction of the cost of employees. In fact it is quite possible to get the work done at no cost if there are enthusiastic contributors willing to donate their effort for free.

Whole books such as *Wikinomics* have already been dedicated to this phenomenon of mass collaboration, but we mention it here because it cannot be ignored in the development of the world of work. In the same way that cheap telecommunications brought about 'offshoring' of call centers in the 1990s, the availability of a worldwide workforce using Web 2.0 technologies is bound to have an impact.

Some of those experiments in moving contact centers to countries such as India proved unsuccessful as customers reacted negatively to language barriers and service levels. Rising wages also reduced the expected cost savings for Western companies using this route. While offshoring to lower-cost centers continues, we are now seeing growth in 'homeshoring', where employed or self-employed individuals work from home doing jobs that otherwise might have been exported abroad.

LiveOps is one such example – a virtual call center business that uses 20,000 independent agents across the US. Maynard Webb, CEO and chairman, expects these new models to run alongside traditional ways of working, rather than replace them.

'Some individuals will still prefer a traditional building in a corporate business park where they go 9–5 every day,' he says. 'I think that is great but I just believe there is so much more we can do as far as defining our work and personal life, and why not consider it? Frankly, that sense of "entrepreneurship", or working on your own terms, is what is behind the start of so many small businesses, great consultants, and the birthplace of even some of the most reputable large businesses. What is assuring to see is that individuals have more options and can choose to contract if they wish.'[4]

In Chapter 2, we looked at this and other new models of networked business where self-employed individuals provide services to clients through a kind of broker organization. As with the use of a contingent workforce by large companies, these new models offer a mix of benefits and potential disadvantages.

On the plus side, they provide great flexibility. Individuals, depending on their income and location constraints, can work at a time and place of their choosing, and for as little or as much time as they want or need. This is effectively self-employment, but with the expectation of a flow of work from the intermediary. For the broker, it is a lower-cost operating model, using contractors only as needed without having to pay salaries or office overheads. Corporate clients get access to skills when they require them without having to employ them directly.

Deployment – providing skills and services where they are needed – is starting to replace employment, according to Caroline Waters, director of people and policy at BT. Some groups of professionals have been working this way for a while. 'Deployment is particularly prevalent in skill areas such as software development.'

The combination of an employed and a contingent workforce provides greater flexibility for business, Waters says. 'You turn the dial up if you need a bit more, be it space or people, and in a downturn you are able to reduce the cost of resource but still retain key skills by giving people access to options such as sabbaticals.'

A socio-economic benefit of online businesses is that they can provide work opportunities for people who would otherwise be excluded from the workforce, for example if they are confined to their homes by disability or by caring for an elderly or sick relative.

On the negative side, the networked business using an agent workforce offers little employment security to the individual. They may well not be covered by employment legislation designed to protect people against exploitation. They will miss out on the employee benefits and job security that go with conventional employment. This is recognized as an issue by the European Union in the Agency Workers Directive, which attempts to close the gap. The EU uses the term 'flexicurity' to denote labor market flexibility combined with worker protection.

There is a danger that unscrupulous employers will exploit contractors in weak bargaining positions. In the transparent world of the Internet, such employers will find it harder to get away with shabby treatment. Nonetheless, there is an important debate to be had, beyond the scope of this book, about what safety nets will be available to the growing numbers of workers outside traditional employment.

Trading the relative security of employment for the freedom of self-employment is likely to attract growing numbers of people who want a different deal from work and who now have the technology at their fingertips to achieve it. It is a trade-off that will inevitably work best for individuals who have the higher skills that are in constant demand, because they will not have to sacrifice earning power.

Given the increasing choice of employment types, we believe that companies keen to attract the best talent will in future have to replicate as many of the benefits of self-employment as possible, while continuing to provide the safety of the employment contract. If they do not, they risk seeing that talent go elsewhere, or go solo.

Careers change shape

It follows from the trends described above that individuals will have to take greater responsibility for keeping their skills up to date and adapting quickly to shifting demand. Online learning will play an increasing role in people's career moves and planning.

Individuals, especially those doing demanding global roles, will have to take responsibility for determining their own boundaries between work and personal life. We see this as a two-way responsibility, since it is also a core duty of managers to ensure that people in their teams are not overworking.

With the rise of women, the arrival of Gen Y and longer working lives, careers will become more fluid and less linear or ladder-shaped. People will have more jobs during their careers, and more careers during their working lives. They may move in and out of formal employment, with spells in self-employment or in hybrid models, such as partial paid employment combined with self-employment or business start-up. There will be a further decline in lifelong loyalty to a single employer, and individuals will rely more heavily on marketing their unique skills, reputation and 'personal brand'.

'Few people will start on a course and stay there throughout their working lives,' says Maynard Webb at LiveOps. 'People will take detours, take time off to raise families, or to learn new skills. I believe that workers will become more well rounded and multi-faceted as a result of this shift.'

Virtual working and measurement by results will enable more diverse styles of leadership to flourish, by removing the anachronism of rewards for long hours spent in the workplace. There will be more women in senior executive roles and on corporate boards, and more senior men and women working in non-traditional patterns, like those we featured in Chapter 5. Online collaboration with teams around the world will give people 'international' experience without necessarily having to relocate.

The digital generation will drive important changes in communication, work and the rhythm of life, according to Damien O'Brien, head of Egon Zehnder International, the executive search firm. 'Rigid 8am to 5pm hours were partly predicated on people needing face-time,' he says. 'This new generation is going to have a different view. That's going to play well to women. A lot of large companies are locked in to tracking employee time, where they're sitting, and what they're doing. That's the old world. I'm confident that in 20 years' time that's going to look very out of date to the vast majority of the world.'[5]

Status and hierarchy

Work status will change. From being defined by job, organization and place in the hierarchy, it will increasingly be about a person's skills, reputation and ability to contribute and build networks. As work becomes more dispersed and less location-dependent, this will be true of status inside organizations as well as among the contingent workforce. The speed of change will depend on national cultural norms, however.

The death of corporate hierarchies has often been predicted, yet many of today's so-called 'flat' organizations still contain hierarchical thinking. However, in organizational cultures that learn how to separate status from hierarchy, the gap between top management and workers, in terms of pay, benefits, personal offices and other trappings of power, will diminish.

Truly flat organizations will be more responsive to social shifts and nimbler in meeting market demands because they will have fewer levels of decision-making and communication barriers.

Throughout this book, we have identified organizations that have inverted the pyramid and put employees first. They have recognized that the role of management is to support front-line employees and help them to generate value for the business. We have spoken to enlightened leaders who earn the respect and loyalty of their employees by listening to them and harnessing their energy. These businesses will adapt and thrive in the new world of work.

This opens up a window of opportunity for the human resource function. Identifying the changes in organizational culture that are coming over the horizon is a key role for senior management. They will be looking to HR professionals for advice on how to make the shift to a 'Type B' culture and engage and invigorate the workforce. For many this will mean a transformation from holding back change and being risk-averse to becoming true business partners and leading the revolution in work practices.

Sustainable developments

The role of offices will shift from being workplaces to meeting places, as described in Chapter 6, and employees will increasingly be categorized by the flexibility and autonomy of their work. Definitions such as 'mobile', 'resident' and 'home-based' will become more common.

More people will work at least part of the time at home, or from work hubs built closer to people's homes, enabling them to work and connect without having to make long commutes.

Already there are significant examples of work hubs in the US and Europe, such as the network of over 100 'smart work centers' across the Netherlands, aimed at cutting traffic jams and pollution on the roads into major cities and increasing work flexibility and balanced lives.[6] These examples will spread. The South Korean government and private companies are to set up hundreds of smart work centers with advanced network and videoconferencing capabilities over the next five years, including some in new housing complexes, according to plans drawn up by the Korea Communications Commission.[7]

Environmental sustainability will continue to be high on the agenda. Industrial Age work has left the planet dangerously polluted, and future work has to be different. In Chapter 6, we looked at how the move to a low carbon economy will drive greater use of remote working and how new office designs are promoting lower energy use and less waste, which in turn generates big cost savings.

As the next generation joins the workforce they will be asking more searching questions about why we work the way we do. They will challenge the need to commute daily and consume the planet's natural resources at the current unsustainable rate. They will be comfortable using videoconferences and video calls, instead of traveling to meetings. And they will be choosing their employers based on their green credentials.

The two young men whose stories we told at the start of this book are not only great examples of future work but also of the new generation's concerns about the future of the planet. In recent years, they say, they have grown increasingly aware that many of the world's problems are interconnected and that current economic systems will lead to more social injustice and environmental destruction.

'We have to change our basic assumptions and systems to keep the earth liveable,' says Martijn van der Linden. 'And this also relates to the way we work.' As well as writing a book on the topic, he has joined the Dutch Platform for an Economy based on Sustainability and Solidarity, while Bram Meulenbeld is advising organizations on how to make sustainable development an integral part of their strategy.

Productivity and growth

In Chapter 4, we explained the big benefits that businesses can derive by moving to 'anytime, anywhere' work. We gave examples of how productivity rises when people are trusted to get on with the job, feel more motivated and suffer fewer distractions from office interruptions or the stresses of commuting.

Productivity is often seen as a job killer because employers are able to produce the same output with fewer workers. However, productivity gains could equally enable organizations to expand with the same number of workers, or to invest in more rapid growth by hiring more workers, with the same expectation of higher productivity from them. When individual businesses are forced to slim down, for example in recessions, productivity gains can keep them afloat and thereby help the wider economy.

A report from the McKinsey Global Institute argues that fears about productivity threatening employment are misconceived. 'In the United States both [productivity and employment] have risen in every ten-year rolling period but one since 1929,' it says. 'Productivity is a job generator rather than a job killer because it not only increases efficiency but can also expand output through innovations that improve the performance, quality, or value of goods and services.'[8]

Conclusion

We are still in the early stages of the transformation of work, largely because corporate cultures and management styles are not keeping pace with technological advances. This was why we embarked on this book: to help managers and organizations make the necessary shift to more efficient business, better lives and a healthier earth for the next generation to inherit.

Future work is one of those rare opportunities for all-round benefit. As we have shown through numerous examples in this book, it contributes positively to the bottom line while improving the lives of workers and helping to protect our fragile ecosystem. It is not an option for business any longer. It is a matter of staying competitive.

As Guy Laurence of Vodafone UK puts it, the leading organizations have adapted fast, but other companies will have to follow suit. The good news is that there are no technological, regulatory or security barriers that cannot be overcome, he says. 'Staff are happier because they don't want to go to the office, you kill fewer trees, and you serve more end-customers. I haven't found any genuine downside other than the dented pride of a few middle managers.'

This book is a call to action for those managers and the leaders of all organizations. If you don't bring your work practices into the twenty-first century, then your employees will react accordingly. The best ones will leave and the remaining ones will be disengaged. Your productivity will drop and in a competitive world other organizations will replace you. If you do, you will not only enjoy bottom line benefits but also be contributing to the wider health of society and the environment.

In recent times, we have seen how Facebook, Twitter and other social media have played a pivotal role in exposing and deposing dictatorships in countries around the world, and watched as regimes have attempted to stifle free speech by controlling internet access. In the world of work, too, we should expect social media to be catalysts of positive change, helping to harness untapped resources of energy and creativity in the workforce.

Management in the new world of work demands a democratic approach in which managers agree the objectives with individuals, provide the tools and then trust them to take responsibility for getting on with it. The trans-formation of work is underway. With this book, we hope that you will be able to make the journey more easily.

Our survey was carried out between June and October 2010 and was aimed at managers from organizations around the world. It was publicized to international alumni of Cass Business School in London and Henley Business School, and to other managers through the authors' networks. There were 366 valid responses submitted online, two-thirds of which were from the business school alumni.

Fifty-one percent of the participants were British and 62 percent were working in the UK. The other respondents represented 38 different nationalities working in 40 countries. Of the participants, 61 percent were male and 39 percent female.

Experience		Age	
Years	%	Years	%
<5	14	<31	4
6–10	30	31–40	47
11–15	22	41–50	34
16–20	14	51–60	13
>20	20	>60	2

Results below are expressed as a percentage of total responses (due to rounding up, not all percentages add up to 100)

Organization Culture									
(AA = definitely A: A = probably A: N = neither: B = probably B: BB = definitely B)									
	Current Organization					Ideal Organization			
	AA	A	N	B	BB	AA	A	N	B	BB
A = People seen as a disposable resource: B = People seen as a long-term investment	8	17	8	33	33	2	3	1	18	75
A = People status conscious, hierarchical: B = All people are equal	26	37	10	17	9	5	16	16	34	29
A = People are closely monitored: B = People take responsibility	8	16	13	41	22	2	4	4	30	60
A = Keep personal life separate: B = Work and personal life intertwined	15	34	12	27	11	16	26	19	27	13

Organization Culture

(AA = definitely A: A = probably A: N = neither: B = probably B: BB = definitely B)

	Current Organization					Ideal Organization				
	AA	A	N	B	BB	AA	A	N	B	BB
A = Work is serious: B = Work is fun	19	31	19	23	8	6	11	14	35	35
A = People need to be directed: B = People are self-motivated	12	25	12	37	14	2	7	4	32	54
A = Bureaucratic, formal: B = Casual, informal	18	21	12	32	18	4	11	16	43	25
A = 'Do what I tell you': B = 'Do the right thing'	9	17	10	36	28	1	3	4	30	61
A = Competitive (between employees): B = Collaborative teamwork	9	15	12	37	27	1	6	6	32	55
A = Cut back on cost: B = Improve effectiveness/ productivity	17	23	9	33	18	2	3	5	21	68
A = Short-term focus: B = Long-term focus	15	26	12	27	20	2	2	7	26	62
A = Low trust in employees: B = High trust in employees	7	18	14	35	25	1	2	3	18	75
A = Rigid: B = Flexible	8	23	13	37	19	2	3	5	30	60
A = Manager only appraisal: B = 360-degree appraisal	30	22	6	20	22	3	4	5	33	56
A = Individual performance pay: B = Team/Organization based pay	24	26	14	18	17	11	17	19	34	20
A = Multi-level hierarchy: B = Flat structure	38	27	4	19	12	6	20	16	38	20
A = Necessary information only: B = Open communications	16	26	10	31	16	2	6	4	31	57
A = Command and control: B = Enable and empower	14	24	10	36	17	2	3	2	27	65
A = Reward time/attendance: B = Reward outcomes/targets	5	12	13	38	32	1	3	1	19	76
A = Keep work in-house: B = Outsource where possible	15	31	21	22	11	9	23	32	23	13
A = Top-down decisions: B = Everyone has a vote	38	39	10	11	2	7	27	27	29	10
A = Managers decide: B = Teams decide	29	45	11	13	2	4	25	21	36	13
A = Follow precedent: B = Be creative	13	33	12	33	10	2	5	7	46	39
A = Multi-level sign-off; B = Freedom to act	32	33	10	18	7	3	11	13	45	27
A = Follow the rules: B = Question the rules	24	35	16	20	5	4	10	13	45	28

(SA = strongly agree: A = agree: N = neither: D = disagree: SD = strongly disagree)

	SA	A	N	D	SD
Communication and influencing skills are essential for good management today	74	23	1	1	2
Good leadership is about empowering people	63	32	3	1	1
I judge my people by their output, not the number of hours they work	48	44	3	3	1
I believe people are more productive given autonomy over their working patterns	35	53	6	6	0
I can trust my people to work on their own	27	60	8	5	1
I believe new ways of working would benefit the business	32	52	10	5	1
I feel I have the right skills to manage a flexible/remote team	20	52	15	12	0
There will be a revolution in working practices in the next decade	28	38	18	14	2
More of my meetings could be held remotely/virtually using IT	16	46	12	22	5
I have never been trained to manage remote/flexible employees	18	42	13	19	9
I would like more freedom to let my people work flexibly	16	42	20	19	4
My organization is not adapting fast enough to new ways of working	20	36	14	26	4
I personally would like more control over where, when and how I do my job	20	35	17	23	5
My organization encourages new ways of working	11	44	19	22	5
People often work flexibly without any formal agreement in my organization	11	44	10	29	7
Many of our meetings are unnecessary	17	34	19	26	5
Senior managers think that the way they have always worked is the right one	14	35	16	28	6
My organization does its best to improve the work–life balance of its people	15	33	23	22	7
My organization effectively implements flexible working arrangements	12	34	22	24	9
Remote workers are more difficult to manage	7	33	21	32	7
My organization rewards long hours and presence in the workplace	9	23	24	31	12
Flexible working is largely seen as a 'women's issue' in our organization	12	19	15	31	24
People who work remotely miss out on promotion	5	24	25	32	14
My role is to monitor my employees closely	3	24	16	43	14
We are losing talented people because of inflexible working arrangements	10	16	20	39	15
We do not have the technology to enable effective remote working	6	17	7	41	29
Flexible working is a luxury in a recession	4	11	16	46	23
I need to see my people face-to-face to know they are working	3	11	15	46	24
People who work at home are poor team players	2	5	17	51	25

NOTES

1 Time for change

1. Interviews by author, October 2009 and January 2011.
2. D. McGregor, *The Human Side of Enterprise* – Annotated Edition (McGraw-Hill, 2006), p. 6.
3. *Government at a Glance 2009,* OECD iLibrary.
4. A. Wittenberg-Cox and A. Maitland, *Why Women Mean Business* (John Wiley & Sons Ltd., 2009).
5. E. Galinsky et al., *Times Are Changing: Gender and Generation at Work and at Home* (Families and Work Institute, 2009).
6. *Working Better Report 2009* (Equality and Human Rights Commission), pp. 10, 20; and M. Shriver, *The Shriver Report: A Woman's Nation Changes Everything* (Center for American Progress, 2009), pp. 162, 415, 442.
7. S. A. Hewlett et al., *Bookend Generations: Leveraging Talent and Finding Common Ground* (Center for Work–Life Policy, New York, 2009).
8. Speech at Northeastern CEO breakfast, 12 November 2008, news@Northeastern.
9. K. Joyce et al., 'Flexible working conditions and their effects on employee health and wellbeing', *Cochrane Database of Systematic Reviews*, no. 2 (2010), Art. No.: CD008009.
10. E. J. Hill et al., 'Workplace flexibility, work hours, and work–life conflict: Finding an extra day or two', *Journal of Family Psychology*, vol. 24, no. 3 (June 2010): 349–358.
11. D. Pennel, 'Change is the only thing that remains constant', *New Europe*, no. 907, 17 October 2010.
12. R. Layard, *Happiness: Lessons from a New Science* (Penguin, 2006).
13. *City & Guilds Happiness Index*, www.cityandguilds.com/24635.html.
14. *Employee Engagement Report 2011* (BlessingWhite Inc. Princeton, NJ).
15. S. A. Hewlett et al., *Bookend Generations: Leveraging Talent and Finding Common Ground* (Center for Work–Life Policy, New York, 2009).
16. *Health and Safety Executive Statistics 2009*, www.hse.gov.uk/statistics/overall/hssh0910.pdf.
17. B. Pocock et al., *How Much Should We Work? Working Hours, Holidays and Working Life: The Participation Challenge, the Australian Work and Life Index 2010* (Centre for Work + Life, University of South Australia, 2010).

18. A. Maitland, 'When managers say: "Suit yourself" ', *Financial Times*, 23 December 2008.
19. *Employee Engagement Report 2011* (BlessingWhite, Inc. Princeton, NJ).
20. Interview with author, November 2010.
21. Op-Ed article by C. Lagarde, *International Herald Tribune*, 10 May 2010.
22. D. H. Pink, *Drive: The Surprising Truth About What Motivates Us* (Canongate Books, 2010).
23. *OECD StatExtracts* (OECD, February 2011).
24. OECD Observer No 266 (OECD, March 2008).
25. Presentation to Henley Knowledge Management Forum, February 2011, by Anand Pillai, senior vice president and global head, Talent Transformation, Intrapreneurship Development & EFCS Transformation Initiatives, HCL Technologies Ltd.

2 How work has evolved

1. P. F. Drucker, 'Managing Knowledge Means Managing Oneself', *Leader to Leader*, vol. 16 (Spring 2000): 8–10.
2. G. Hamel, *The Future of Management* (Harvard Business School Press, 2007).
3. Interview with author, December 2010.
4. U. Hotopp, 'Teleworking in the UK', *ONS Labour Market Trends*, vol. 110, no. 6, p. 311.
5. *Telework Trendlines 2009*, A survey brief by WorldatWork commissioned from The Dieringer Research Group.
6. *Crackberry is the 2006 Word of the Year* (PRNewswire, 1 November 2006).
7. *Managing Tomorrow's People – Where will you be in 2020?* (PwC UK, 2010).
8. A. Richman et al., *Innovative Workplace Flexibility Options for Hourly Workers* (Corporate Voices for Working Families, 2009).
9. *Generation Y: Realising the Potential* (A joint research paper by ACCA and Mercer, July 2010).
10. *Working Life: Employee Attitudes and Engagement 2006* (CIPD).
11. Maternity at Work: A review of National Legislation/International Labour Office, Conditions of Work and Employment Programme Second edition (Geneva: ILO, 2010), p. 68.
12. *Failing its Families: Lack of Paid Leave and Work–Family Supports in the US* (Human Rights Watch, 23 February 2011).
13. *Global Education Digest* (UNESCO, 2009).
14. E. Galinsky, K. Aumann, J. Bond, *Times are Changing: Gender and Generation at Work and at Home* (Families and Work Institute 2008 National Study of the Changing Workforce).

15. *Working Better, Meeting the Changing Needs of Families, Workers and Employers in the 21st Century* (Equality and Human Rights Commission, 2009).
16. S. A. Hewlett et al., *Bookend Generations: Leveraging Talent and Finding Common Ground* (Center for Work–Life Policy, 2009).
17. *Working Better: The over 50s, the New Work Generation* (Equality and Human Rights Commission, 2010).
18. G. Magnus, *The Age of Aging, How Demographics are Changing the Global Economy and Our World* (John Wiley & Sons, 2009), p. xxii.
19. Being an agent FAQ, LiveOps website, March 2011.
20. Interview with author, December 2010.
21. Interview with author, October 2010.

3   Turning convention on its head

1. Apple Supplier Responsibility, 2011 Progress Report: http://images.apple.com/supplierresponsibility/pdf/Apple_SR_2011_Progress_Report.pdf.
2. K. Hille, 'Chinese pay rises spur move to cheaper sites', *Financial Times* (25 June 2010).
3. Name changed to protect identity.
4. Chart adapted from *Enter the Timelords: Transforming Work to Meet the Future* (Equal Opportunities Commission/Equality and Human Rights Commission, March 2008).
5. T. Harnish and K. Lister, *Results Based Management* (Telework Research Network, 2010).
6. C. Ressler and J. Thompson, *Why Work Sucks and How to Fix It* (Portfolio, 2008).
7. Information provided by Ryan in response to authors' request, July 2010.
8. D. McGregor, *The Human Side of Enterprise* (McGraw-Hill, 1960).
9. More information on W L Gore can be found in G. Hamel, *The Future of Management* (Boston: The Harvard Business School Press, 2007), pp. 83–100.
10. G. Hamel, *The Future of Management* (Harvard Business Press, 2007).
11. D. Pink, *Drive: The Surprising Truth about What Motivates Us* (Canongate, 2010), p. 73.
12. R. Wooten et al., 'A Joint US–UK Study of Home Telenursing', *Journal of Telemedicine and Telecare*, vol. 4, no. 1 (1998): 83–85.
13. R. Semler, *Maverick* (Random House Business, 2001).
14. The Happy Manifesto: 9 Steps to a Great Workplace, 5 November 2010, http://www.happy.co.uk/the-happy-manifesto-9-steps-to-a-great-workplace/

4   Why it makes business sense

1. Speaking at the White House Workplace Flexibility Forum, 31 March 2010.
2. Interview with author, August 2010.
3. Case study in *Working Better: A Managers' Guide to Flexible Working* (Equality and Human Rights Commission, October 2009).
4. A. Maitland, 'When managers say: suit yourself', *Financial Times* (22 December 2008).
5. Data supplied by Chubb, 2008 and 2011.
6. *A New Way of Working, Insights from Global Leaders* (IBM Institute for Business Value, April 2010).
7. Data provided by Cisco, August 2010.
8. P. Thomson, *Working at Home: The Productivity Tool of the Future* (Telework Association, February 2010).
9. Microsoft 2010 US Remote Working Research Summary: National Survey Findings.
10. Interview with authors, August 2010.
11. *Flexible Working and Performance* (Cranfield University School of Management and Working Families, 2008).
12. Interview with Gary Kildare, VP, Human Resources, IBM, June 2010, and J. Caldow *Working Outside the Box, A Study of the Growing Momentum in Telework* (Institute for Electronic Government, IBM, 2009).
13. Interview with authors, March 2011.
14. Swine flu briefing (Business continuity planning section), Institute of Directors, March 2010.
15. M. Virtanen et al., 'Overtime work and incident coronary heart disease: the Whitehall II prospective cohort study', *European Heart Journal*, vol. 31, no. 14 (2010), pp. 1737–1744.
16. S. A. Hewlett and C. B. Luce, 'Extreme Jobs: The Dangerous Allure of the 70-Hour Workweek', *Harvard Business Review* (December 2006). Also, S. A. Hewlett, 'Extreme managers need protection', *Financial Times*, 28 November 2006.
17. J. Sundquist et al., 'Psychosocial working conditions and self-reported long-term illness: a population-based study of Swedish-born and foreign-born employed persons', *Ethnicity & Health*, vol. 8, no. 4 (2003): 307–317.
18. A. Tsutsumi et al., 'Low Control at Work and the Risk of Suicide in Japanese Men: A Prospective Cohort Study', *Psychotherapy and Psychosomatics*, vol. 76, no. 3 (2007): 177–185.
19. Interview with author, June 2010.
20. Interviews with author, July 2010 and February 2011.

21. Interview with authors, July 2010.
22. *Working Better: A Managers' Guide to Flexible Working* (Equality and Human Rights Commission, 2009).
23. *Green: Empowering People to Heal the Planet* (Cisco).
24. Telework Research Network, June 2010, www.teleworkresearchnetwork.com.
25. *Broadband Services: Economic and Environmental Benefits* (American Consumer Institute, Center for Citizen Research, 2007).
26. Lister, K. and Harnish, T., 'The Shifting Nature of Work in the UK: Bottom Line Benefits of Telework' (Telework Research Network, February 2011).
27. Interview with author, August 2010.

5   Leaders of the future

1. Interviews with author, January and September 2010.
2. Interview with author, August 2010.
3. Speaking at The Conference Board Diversity & Inclusion Conference, Chicago, 13 May 2009.
4. European Foundation for the Improvement of Living and Working Conditions, *Part-Time Work in Europe, European Company Survey 2009* (Publications Office of the European Union, 2011), p. 26.
5. Equality and Human Rights Commission, *Working Better: Meeting the Changing Needs of Families, Workers and Employers in the 21st Century* (EHRC, March 2009), p. 60.
6. H. Ibarra and O. Obodaru, 'Women and the Vision Thing', *Harvard Business Review*, vol. 87, no. 1, (January 2009) pp. 62–70.
7. ILM/MT, *Index of Leadership Trust 2010* (Institute of Leadership and Management, 2010), p. 11.
8. C. Mitchell and D. Learmond, *Go Where There Be Dragons, Leadership Essentials for 2020 and Beyond,* Council Perspectives (The Conference Board, 2010).
9. Interview with author, July 2010.
10. Speaking at Out of Office conference, Opportunity Now, London, 22 June 2010.
11. R. Fry and D'V. Cohn, *New Economics of Marriage: The Rise of Wives* (Pew Research Center, 2010).
12. Brookfield (formerly GMAC) 2010 Global Relocation Trends Survey.
13. Interview with author, July 2010.
14. Cited in: Equality and Human Rights Commission, *Working Better: Meeting the Changing Needs of Families, Workers and Employers in the 21st Century* (EHRC, 2009), p. 67.

15. A. Maitland, 'Calling time on hours', *Financial Times*, 5 November 2008.
16. Interview with author, September 2010.
17. Interview with author, July 2010.

6 Changing workplaces

1. Speaking during a visit to the Netherlands office, January 2010, and in subsequent online and telephone interviews with author, October 2010.
2. Microsoft video: http://mediadl.microsoft.com/mediadl/www/n/netherlands/pers/Film_Sevil_Peach.wmv.
3. *The Cisco Connected World Report* (Cisco, 2010), http://newsroom.cisco.com/dlls/2010/ekits/ccwr_final.pdf.
4. Interview with author, November 2010.
5. Interview with author, October 2010.
6. *Microsoft Continues its Redmond Headquarters Expansion on a Grand Scale* (Microsoft News Center, 12 November 2007).
7. Interview by Janne Ryan for the Australian Broadcasting Corporation's By Design program, 16 September 2009.
8. Office of Personnel Management, *Status of Telework in the Federal Government* (OPM, 2009).
9. S. Losey, '1 Million More Teleworkers: Can Agencies Turn New Legislation into Reality?', *Federal Times* (29 November 2010).
10. Interview with author, December 2010.
11. M. Dixon and P. Ross, *Agility @ Work* (Unwired Ventures Ltd., 2010), p. 14.
12. A. Maitland, 'No Space Wasted in the Velcro Workplace of the Future', *Financial Times*, 7 November 2008, and interview with author, January 2011.
13. Interview with authors, July 2010.
14. 'Business Diary: Matt Brittin', *Financial Times*, 27 September 2010.
15. Interview with author, December 2010.

7 Culture is critical

1. V. Nayar, *Employees First, Customers Second* (Harvard Business Press, 2010), p. 169.
2. *Women Matter 2: Female Leadership, a Competitive Edge for the Future* (McKinsey & Co, 2008) and H. Ibarra and O. Obodaru, 'Women and the Vision Thing', *Harvard Business Review*, vol. 87, no. 1. (January 2009), pp. 62–70.
3. A. Wittenberg-Cox and A. Maitland, *Why Women Mean Business* (Wiley, 2009), pp. 2–3.
4. A. Maitland, 'Workspace: The Other Gender', *The Conference Board Review*, vol. XLVII, no. 1 (Winter 2010), pp. 68–69.

5. Interviews with author, June and September 2010.
6. Interview with author, February 2011.
7. Interview with authors, August 2010.
8. *Balancing Work and Family, A Practical Guide to Help Organizations Meet the Global Workforce Challenge* (HRD Press, 2010).
9. Average usual weekly hours worked on the main job, 2009 (Organization for Economic Cooperation and Development).
10. Eurostat Labor Force Survey 2009, cited in *Part-Time Work in Europe, 2009* (European Foundation for the Improvement of Living and Working Conditions).
11. Interview with author, January 2011.
12. Interview with author, January 2011.
13. *Working Better: Meeting the Changing Needs of Families, Workers and Employers in the 21st Century* (Equality and Human Rights Commission, UK, 2009).
14. Statistics from The Netherlands Institute for Social Research.
15. K. Tong-hyung, 'Wireless Technologies to Allow Workers to Stay at Home', *The Korea Times* (20 July 2010).
16. Average usual weekly hours worked on the main job, 2009, and OECD estimates of labour productivity levels, 2009 (Organization for Economic Cooperation and Development).
17. A. Wittenberg-Cox and A. Maitland, *Why Women Mean Business* (Wiley, 2009), pp. 193–200.
18. Employee Engagement Report 2011 (BlessingWhite Inc, 2011).
19. Interview with author, January 2011.
20. Interviews with author, November 2010.

8 How to break free of the old model

1. Speaking at the Linkage Inc. Women in Leadership Summit, 8 November 2010, and interview with author.
2. Interview with authors, August 2010.
3. A. Maitland, *Working Better: A Managers' Guide to Flexible Working* (Equality and Human Rights Commission, 2009) and interview with author, December 2010.
4. Interview with authors, July 2010.
5. Interview with authors, March 2011.
6. A. Maitland, *Working Better: A Managers' Guide to Flexible Working* (Equality and Human Rights Commission, 2009).
7. A. Maitland, 'Fathers & Daughters', *Management Today* (November 2009).
8. Interviews with author, June and September 2010.

9. Interview with authors, August 2010.
10. P. Thomson, *Tomorrow's Leaders* (City and Guilds, 2007).
11. Interview with author, November 2010.

9   Putting it into practice

1. Interview with author, August, 2010.
2. Interview with author, September 2010.
3. *Whistle – but Don't Tweet – While You Work*, Robert Half Technology (2009).
4. Interview with authors, August 2010.
5. Interview with authors, August 2010.
6. Interview with author, August 2010.
7. Interview with author, January 2011.
8. *Working Better: A Managers' Guide to Flexible Working* (Equality and Human Rights Commission, 2009).
9. Interview with author, October 2010.
10. Interview with author, June 2010.

10   Looking over the horizon

1. *Worldwide Internet Usage and Commerce, 2009–20013 Forecast* (IDC, 2009).
2. Interview with authors, March 2011.
3. *How HR Can Save a Million Dollars or More* (Human Capital Institute, 27 October 2009).
4. Interview by email with author, December 2010.
5. Interview with author, November 2010.
6. ' "Smart work" could be key to green growth', *EurActiv Network*, 28 February 2011.
7. 'Wireless technologies to allow workers to stay at home', *The Korea Times*, 20 July 2010.
8. D. Hunt, J. Manyika and J. Remes, McKinsey Global Institute, 'Why US productivity can grow *without* killing jobs: Private-sector innovation and the spread of best practices can raise growth rates and spur employment', *McKinsey Quarterly*, February 2011.

FURTHER READING

Benko, C. and Weisberg, A. (2007) *Mass Career Customization*, Harvard Business School Press.

Birkinshaw, J. (2010) *Reinventing Management*, John Wiley & Sons.

Brake, T. (2009) *Where in the World is My Team?*, Jossey-Bass.

Donkin, R. (2010) *The Future of Work*, Palgrave Macmillan.

Drucker, P. F. (1999) *Management Challenges for the 21st Century*, Butterworth-Heinemann.

Hamel, G. (2007) *The Future of Management*, Harvard Business School Press.

Handy, C. (2001) *The Elephant and the Flea*, Hutchinson.

Heil, G., Bennis, W., Stephens, D. (2000) *Douglas McGregor, Revisited*, John Wiley & Sons.

Layard, R. (2006) *Happiness: Lessons from a New Science*, Penguin.

Malone, T. W. (2004) *The Future of Work*, Harvard Business School Press.

McGregor, D. (2006) *The Human Side of Enterprise – Annotated Edition*, McGraw-Hill.

Magnus, G. (2009) *The Age of Aging*, John Wiley & Sons.

Nayar, V. (2010) *Employees First, Customers Second*, Harvard Business Press.

Pink, D. H. (2010) *Drive*, Canongate Books.

Ressler, C. and Thompson, J. (2008) *Why Work Sucks and How to Fix It*, Penguin Group.

Semler, R. (2001) *Maverick*, Random House Business.

Semler, R. (2003) *The Seven-Day Weekend*, Arrow Books.

Shirky, C. (2008) *Here Comes Everybody*, Penguin.

Tapscott, D. (2009) *Grown Up Digital*, McGraw-Hill.

Wittenberg-Cox, A. and Maitland, A. (2009) *Why Women Mean Business*, John Wiley & Sons.

Wittenberg-Cox, A. (2010) *How Women Mean Business*, John Wiley & Sons.

Index